the
revolt
in
tibet

by FRANK MORAES

Report on Mao's China
Jawaharlal Nehru: A Biography
Yonder One World: A Study of Asia and the West
The Revolt in Tibet

the
revolt
in
tibet

FRANK MORAES

the macmillan company   new york   1960

Second Printing 1960

The Macmillan Company, New York
Brett-Macmillan Ltd., Galt, Ontario

Printed in the United States of America

Library of Congress catalog card number: 60-6644

for
peter
and
lily

foreword

Communist China's brutal seizure of Tibet has roused revulsion and indignation throughout the free countries of
Asia and in the democratic world. This book deals with the
events in Tibet which led finally to the Dalai Lama's flight,
and with the relations between China and Tibet. It also offers
a brief survey of Tibet's history and people, together with
an assessment of the impact made by the Communist aggression in Asia, particularly on India.

FRANK MORAES

contents

the
revolt
in
tibet

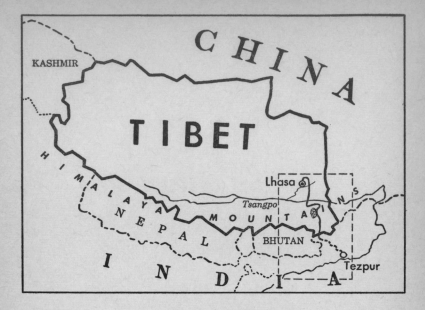

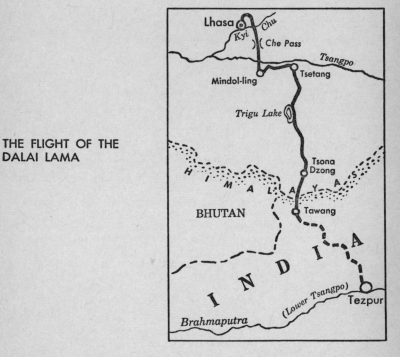

**THE FLIGHT OF THE
DALAI LAMA**

flight
from
lhasa

CHAPTER ONE

A gray-brown mist of swirling sand enveloped the Norbulingka, summer abode of the Dalai Lama at Lhasa. It was
the evening of March 17, 1959.

All that morning, while the Kashag * and the Tsongdu †
debated whether the twenty-four-year-old God-king should
leave Lhasa, the sun had shone brightly on the tiled roofs
of the massive gateways and on the poplars in the gay green
park and gardens surrounding the palace. Inside the palace
the members of the Tsongdu and the Kashag had been debat-
ing since March 11th whether Tibet's stability and the Dalai

---

* The Tibetan Cabinet comprising six ministers, two of them monks. They
are appointed by the Dalai Lama, and outwardly the Kashag is the supreme
administrative body. The six ministers are known as *shapes* or *kalons,* but
the monks who are the senior members are called Kalon Lamas. The four
lay members are nobles.

† The Tsongdu is the National, or Grand, Assembly, a nominated body
comprising 350 high officials, including the abbots of the three Great Monasteries of Drepung, Sera, and Ganden, whose views have great authority. The
Tsongdu meets whenever important matters are referred to it by the Dalai
Lama or the Kashag.

Lama's safety lay in yielding to the increasingly peremptory threats of the Chinese or in flight.

The crisis, simmering for some months, had boiled over on March 10th. About four weeks earlier the Dalai Lama had agreed to attend a cultural show in the auditorium of the Chinese military headquarters at Lhasa. This was in no way abnormal; for, although relations between him and the Chinese authorities had grown cool since he had evaded their demand to deploy his bodyguard of five thousand men against the rebellious Khamba tribesmen, who had been engaged in intermittent guerrilla warfare against the Chinese for over three years, their dealings with each other had been polite and even superficially cordial. By February the warlike Khambas, whose revolt began late in 1955 in the district of Kanze in the border region of Szechwan, had spilled over the Sino-Tibetan frontier, and were harassing Chinese outposts within less than fifty miles of Lhasa. Chinese efforts to inveigle the Living Buddha into moving his troops against them had failed. A showdown was inevitable.

It came early in the first week of March when a letter from Lieutenant General Tan Kuan-san, political commissar of the Chinese Army units in Tibet, was delivered with calculated indifference to Tibetan protocol, directly to the Dalai Lama. It curtly called on the God-king to present himself unescorted at the Chinese military headquarters of General Chang Ching-wu, the Peking Government's representative in Tibet. There was consternation at the Norbulingka when the contents of the letter became known. It was unheard of that a communication should go directly to the Dalai Lama instead of being respectfully submitted, as usage demanded, through the Kashag. To order His Holiness to appear unescorted was near-blasphemy, since religion and ceremonial required that the Living Buddha should not move in public without his train of senior abbots and courtiers. What was behind the Chinese demand? The suspicion grew in Tibetan minds that the purpose was to abduct the Dalai Lama, isolate him from his advisers and people, and use him as a helpless instrument to advance Chinese policies and designs in Tibet.

Lhasa's streets that week were teeming with crowds gathered to celebrate the Tibetan New Year, and among them were many hundreds of Khamba tribesmen who had made their way into the capital. It was not long before news of General Tan's letter to the Dalai Lama reached the milling mob. Among the first to hear the news from the Norbulingka was Gyusm Chemo,* fifty-seven-year-old mother of the Dalai Lama, and her distress infected the crowds in the streets, which were soon filled with wailing women. On March 12th a procession of Tibetan women waited on the Indian consul general, whose official residence, midway between the Potala, the Dalai Lama's winter palace, and the Norbulingka, was to be damaged a few days later by Chinese mortar and artillery fire directed at these two targets. The women requested the Indian representative to accompany them to the Chinese Foreign Bureau and be a witness while they presented their demands. Quite properly the consul general expressed his inability to do so, but undertook to bring such matters to the notice of the Chinese authorities.

Meanwhile, on March 10th, as news of the Chinese communication to the Dalai Lama spread through Lhasa, a vast crowd estimated at about thirty thousand surrounded the Norbulingka, demanding that His Holiness should on no account expose himself to the risk of visiting the Chinese military headquarters. The Tibetans made no secret of their deep hostility to the Chinese. Tibetan officials and army personnel arrested Communist sympathizers, and anti-Chinese manifestoes were openly distributed. Arms and ammunition secreted in the monasteries and other hiding places were

* Meaning Great Mother.

passed out to the populace, including the Khamba warriors who strutted the streets, their feet encased in great shaggy boots, their bodies bristling with rifles, daggers, and swords, and accompanied by lean, savage dogs. Those suspected of collaboration with the Chinese were given short shrift. Sampo Tsewong-rentzen, deputy commander of the Tibet military area command and a member of the Kashag, was attacked and wounded but escaped death. Significantly, he and Ngapo Ngawang Jigme, who was also strongly pro-Chinese in his sympathies, were the only two members of the Kashag who stayed behind in Tibet when the Dalai Lama fled to India. Another collaborationist, a monk known as Lama Pebala Soanamchiato, was less fortunate. He was lynched by a furious crowd, and his corpse was dragged ignominiously by the feet through the streets.

Faced with these demonstrations of defiance and open hostility, the Chinese grew nervous. They could rely on very few Tibetans, and they knew that even the local Tibetan Army of a little over three thousand men, under the control of the Dalai Lama's government, sympathized with the rebels. With three hundred thousand of their own troops in Tibet, and with many thousands more available should the need arise, the Chinese could never have doubted the ultimate outcome. In arms and equipment they were also vastly superior. But for the vehemence and violence of Tibetan hostility they were not prepared, and it shook them badly. Nervously they set up machine-gun posts, reinforced their numbers in Lhasa, and trained their artillery on the Potala and the Norbulingka.

Inside the Norbulingka the Dalai Lama and his advisers played for time. They too could have no illusions about the outcome. Though the majority of the National Assembly was in favor of the Dalai Lama leaving Lhasa, a few were hesitant, some of them genuinely concerned as to whether it would not be wiser in the interests of Tibet and His Holiness if the God-king stayed on. Others, with their loyalties divided between the Dalai Lama and the Chinese authorities, were of two minds, and urged caution. On March 17th the Chinese themselves brought matters to a head when in a foolish attempt to intimidate the Dalai Lama and his advisers they lobbed a couple of mortar shells into the grounds of the Norbulingka which fell harmlessly into a pond. The shells helped to make up the mind of the National Assembly, which decided to advise the Dalai Lama to leave Lhasa.

In the crucial six days between March 11th and March 17th the Living Buddha, though outwardly serene, and content to leave any decision concerning himself to his advisers, had not been idle. To allay Chinese suspicions that the demonstrations around the Norbulingka on March 10th were organized, the Dalai Lama entered into a correspondence with General Tan Kuan-san in the course of which six letters were exchanged between the two. The authenticity of these letters was originally questioned—among others, by India's prime minister, Mr. Nehru—but there can now be no doubt that they were genuine, and written by the God-king with calculated purpose, as he himself admitted to Mr. Nehru. On March 10th His Holiness in a letter to the general explained that he was prevented from coming to the Chinese headquarters by the crowds who besieged his summer palace. The general's letters are dated March 10th, 11th, and 15th, and the second of these is icily polite but minatory in tone. From addressing the God-king as "Respected Dalai Lama" in his letter of March 10th, the general changes to a curt "Dalai Lama" in his letter of March 11th. He reverts to the recognized form of address in his last letter, but the threats grow more insistent. Following his first letter, the Dalai Lama wrote to the general on March 11th and again on March 12th, signing the last communication not with the customary "Dalai Lama" but merely "Dalai." In all of these letters, however, the God-king attempted to soothe Chinese susceptibilities and suspicions by describing in the stylized Communist phraseology the crowds who prevented him from leaving his palace as "reactionary evil elements" and "the reactionary clique" whose "unlawful actions . . . break my heart." While his advisers debated the question of his flight, the Dalai Lama was stalling.

When finally, in the afternoon of March 17th, the Kashag and Tsongdu decided that the Living Buddha should leave, it was agreed that the decision should be conveyed to His Holiness by a small delegation which included the three abbots of the Great Monasteries of Drepung, Sera, and Ganden, who had taken a prominent part in the discussions. The Dalai Lama received them with his accustomed serenity, his tall loose-jointed figure wrapped in the customary wine-red cashmere toga, his right shoulder bare as custom also ordains. They bowed reverently before him and conveyed their advice urging him to leave. Their average age was at least twice that of the twenty-four-year-old God-king. His Holiness listened calmly to their pleas but seemed momentarily hesitant.

"I shall go," he said, "if by going I can help my people and not merely save my life."

At this the delegation prostrated itself at the God-king's feet, pleading with him to leave, and to leave immediately.

"Your Holiness must go before it is too late."

The upturned corners of the Dalai Lama's mouth curved in the boyish, strangely wistful smile which the world now knows.

"If that is your unanimous wish, I shall go."

Sunlight shone on the courtyards and filtered through the trees of the wooded gardens and pathways surrounding the palace. It was decided that the God-king, accompanied by his mother, sister, and brother, his tutors, cabinet ministers, and senior officials, should leave within a few hours. As evening came, even before night had descended, a sandstorm swept Lhasa, enveloping the Norbulingka behind a curtain of gritty sand and dust. Conditions could not have been more ideal for the God-king's escape.

Outside, the restive crowds, by now increasingly militant, milled around the palace where it was known that the Kashag and the Tsongdu were in session. In his letter of March 11th Tan had complained to the Dalai Lama that the rebels were "openly and arrogantly" carrying out "military provocations" by posting machine guns and armed personnel "along the national defense highway north of the Norbulingka." The Dalai Lama in his reply dated March 12th, while admitting some minor incidents, attempted to appease the general. "I am making every possible effort to deal with them," he assured him. "At eight-thirty this morning a few Tibetan Army men suddenly fired several shots near the Chinghai-Tibet highway. Fortunately, no serious disturbances occurred." It was evident that the Tibetans, military and civilian, were in an ugly mood.

Even before the final decision was taken, preparations had been made for the Living Buddha's departure. Food had been stocked, and part of the treasure at the Dalai Lama's command was packed on a train of mules. Apart from the sandstorm, the celebration of the Little New Year festival, when groups moved about the streets, facilitated the royal party's escape. It was agreed that the party should split up into small groups, leaving the palace separately, and meet at Nethang, thirty-five miles south of Lhasa, between the river Kyi Chu, one of whose tributaries skirts the southern rim of the Norbulingka, and the river Tsangpo, as the Brahmaputra is known in Tibet.

From Lhasa to the Indian border is about 150 air miles,

but the route traversed by the Dalai Lama covered about three hundred miles across some of the world's most treacherous mountain territory, over rivers and through valleys and snow-covered passes. The fifteen-day trek was accomplished on foot, by horseback, on mules, and by inflated yak-skin coracles, the party moving at a pace of around twenty miles a day. The route lay across the river Kyi Chu, up the 17,000-foot-high Che Pass, and then down over the other side of the mountain range to the river Tsangpo. South of the Tsangpo the terrain varies between open plateau and inhospitable mountains, and there the Dalai Lama's party was enabled to move from village to village because the territory was controlled by the Khambas. Once the party emerged from the Brahmaputra Valley they were comparatively safe, for the Loka Province, the Yarlung Valley, and the district of Tsona Dzong were studded with rebel strongholds, among them Mindol-ling, thirty-five miles from the south bank of the Tsangpo, and others strung in the region of Lake Trigu. From then on, the dramatic race down from the Roof of the World to the Indian border more or less followed the ancient caravan trail to Tawang.

Throughout the evening of March 17th members of the National Assembly, cabinet ministers, and other officials trickled out of the Norbulingka in groups of three or four. They included the Dalai Lama's mother, his twenty-six-year-old sister, Tsering Domme, and his younger brother, fourteen-year-old Ngari Rimpoche. Also in the party were his two tutors, the senior of them being the erudite, grave-faced Trichang Rimpoche, and three cabinet ministers—Surkong Wonching-galei, Neusha Thibten-tarpa, and Hsika Jigme-dorje. The fourth member of the Kashag, Yuto Chahsi-dongehu, had fled to India as far back as 1956. In addition to the ministers and officials were lesser monks and a retinue of servants, the party numbering around ninety.

With the crowds in the streets and byways surrounding the

Norbulingka were soldiers of the Tibetan Army and scores of stray Khambas who provided a protective screen to the royal party against the inquisitive gaze of the Chinese soldiers garrisoned about three hundred yards from the walls of the palace. The Khambas had been instructed to start a diversionary movement should the Chinese discover the flight of the Dalai Lama, and the commander of the Tensung Khamba Regiment had been alerted. The Chinese, however, suspected nothing and had no idea of what was afoot. It had been arranged that a detachment of twenty-five soldiers from the Dalai Lama's personal bodyguard, the Kusung Regiment, should accompany the party. South of the Tsangpo they would be met by another squad of Khamba tribesmen, who would take over from the God-king's personal bodyguard the duty of protecting him.

Around 10:00 P.M. the Dalai Lama, accompanied by three attendants, emerged from the south gate of the palace. He had discarded his spectacles, and wore the garb of a poor monk, consisting of a russet-brown *chuba,* or loose mantle, with a stocking cap not unlike a balaklava, swathing his face against the sandstorm. The Tibetans call this cap *o-mo-su.* He walked nonchalantly through the gate and on to the street, with no one even glancing at him.

"His Holiness left the palace just as if he were taking a normal walk," one of the attendants remarked later. "No one interfered. No one tried to stop us."

In the dry bed of the tributary of the river Kyi Chu was an encampment of Chinese soldiers alongside which the Dalai Lama had to walk. Here again his luck held. The sandstorm still blew across Lhasa, and through its haze the royal party passed unnoticed and unrecognized. At the Kyi Chu crossing point the Living Buddha and his attendants boarded the public ferry together with a score of other passengers. No one recognized him.

On the other bank horses were waiting, ready and saddled

for the royal party. Mounting, the four disappeared into the night. By midnight the various groups had reached their rendezvous at Nethang. From there the party proceeded on horseback to the Che Pass, dismounting at the summit and walking down to the valley of the Tsangpo. It is a Tibetan custom to ride uphill but to walk downhill. An old Tibetan jingle runs:

> Kyan-la mi chi-na, ta omen:
> Tur-la mi pap-na, mi-men.
> (If you do not carry him up a hill, you're no horse.
> If you do not walk down the hill, you're no man.)

At early dawn the Dalai Lama was ferried across the river in a yak-skin coracle, and again awaiting the party on the other bank were horses saddled for the long ride ahead. Here they were in comparatively safe territory, for the Khamba tribesmen controlled a large sector of southeast Tibet below the Tsangpo. So hurried, however, was their departure from Lhasa that it was not possible to give advance warning to the villages and forts through which the Dalai Lama passed, and only after two days' travel was the party met by an escort of Khamba tribesmen who replaced the God-king's personal bodyguard. As the party moved, requests for fresh horses were sent ahead by the Tibetan "arrow service," a highly efficient system which ensures that messages under the Dalai Lama's seal are dispatched by couriers on horseback who in the manner of a relay race hand them over from courier to courier until they reach their destination.

News of the Living Buddha's presence soon seeped through the area, and at various points he was met by reverential crowds who bowed or prostrated themselves before him. Contrary to general belief the party traveled largely by day. It was essential that no time should be lost, since the Chinese were bound to discover the fact of the Dalai Lama's flight within a day or two of his departure. Actually, they did so on March 19th while the royal party was between Mindol-ling and Tsetang where the Khamba tribesmen took over the duty of protecting the God-king.

Having negotiated the grueling 17,000-foot Che Pass which separates the Lhasa Valley from the plain of the Brahmaputra, the Dalai Lama's party found itself not only in friendly territory but on less difficult terrain. South of this broad plain was more broken country, but the Khambas were loyal escorts and good guides. The original plan, on crossing the Tsangpo, was to make for the semi-independent border kingdom of Bhutan, but on hearing that the Chinese had blown up bamboo and rope bridges spanning mountain streams near the frontier of Bhutan it was decided to seek refuge in India.

From Tsetang, capital of Loka Province, to the Indian border is approximately one hundred miles. When on March 19th the Chinese realized that the Dalai Lama had fled, they were infuriated. But by then they must have realized that His Holiness was beyond the Brahmaputra, in Khamba-controlled territory, and that no practical purpose would be served by sending columns in pursuit of him. Moreover, their hands were full. At Lhasa and elsewhere in Tibet the hostility of the Tibetans had erupted into open violence, and following the departure of the Dalai Lama the Tibetans intensified their anti-Chinese activities, destroying bridges, erecting road blocks, setting fire to Chinese buildings, and surrounding units of the Red forces. One of the last acts of the Kashag before leaving Lhasa was to denounce the Sino-Tibetan agreement of May 23, 1951, whereunder Tibet, in return for Chinese recognition of Tibetan national regional autonomy, had conceded Peking's right to control her foreign relations and had acknowledged "the unified leadership of the Central People's Government." This repudiation was provoked by persistent violations of the agreement by the Chinese, of whom the Tibetan Government now demanded that the Chinese withdraw their occupation forces since Tibet in view of these violations considered herself independent. Though the declaration was never officially delivered to the Chinese authorities, the Tibetans adopted it as a charter of independence, and on March 12th a women's procession attempted to deposit it at the Chinese Foreign Bureau in Lhasa.

Open rebellion broke out in the Tibetan capital on the night of March 19th when the Dalai Lama's bodyguard, the Kusung Regiment, along with the Trapchi Regiment and units of the Gyantse Regiment, launched armed attacks against the People's Liberation Army garrison. They were assisted by monks, who took a prominent part in the rebellion, and by other individuals to whom arms had been distributed. The Chinese put the total number of the rebels at around twenty thousand, their own number in Lhasa being estimated at forty thousand. Fighting began in earnest the next day when the Chinese trained their artillery on the Potala and Norbulingka palaces and on several monasteries, including Drepung and Sera, and on the great temple of the "Jo," or Lord Buddha, called the Jokhang, which has been described as the Lateran of Lamaism. All these ancient edifices were damaged, some badly, and hundreds of priceless treasures and manuscripts were destroyed. The official residence of the Indian consul general, between the Potala and the Norbulingka, being in the line of fire, was slightly damaged. It houses the only foreign wireless transmitter in Lhasa with access to the free world, which is perhaps one reason why the Chinese were anxious to see the Indian consular personnel vacate it during the fighting. The consul general declined.

Of the final outcome there could be no doubt. By March 22nd the Chinese had succeeded in putting down the Lhasa revolt; they claimed to have taken four thousand Tibetan prisoners and to have seized eight thousand small arms, over one hundred heavier weapons, including machine guns, mortars, and mountain guns, and 10 million bullets. The Chinese estimate of Tibetans killed is two thousand, though figures vary, some placing the total closer to five thousand. But in northern and northeastern Tibet, as in the area south of the Tsangpo, scattered rebel forces held out.

The Chinese were particularly vengeful toward the monks, concentrating on the monasteries, among them Rongbuk on the northern face of Mount Everest, which they surrounded with about four hundred soldiers. Mass deportations of Tibetans from Lhasa were also reported, one estimate giving the number at around fifteen thousand. Savage reprisals were inflicted on loyal Tibetans, and a large number of them were summarily executed.

Traders and refugees to India brought tales of Chinese attempts to launch an offensive south of the Brahmaputra in the region of Nagartse, east of Gyantse, where the Khamba rebels have some strongholds around Yamdrok Lake. The Sikang-Lhasa road, built by the Chinese, extends west from the Tibetan capital to Shigatse, seat of the Panchen Lama,* and from there to Gyantse, which lies on the trade route from Lhasa to Gangtok, capital of the semi-independent frontier state of Sikkim, a neighbor of Bhutan. Gyantse is about one hundred miles southwest of Lhasa. Dr. Satyanarain Sinha, a former member of the Lok Sabha (Lower House of Parliament †), who was trekking in the southern regions of Tibet around this time, claimed that some Khambas had told

* The Panchen Lama, who is twenty-two, and tenth of his line, is second only to the Dalai Lama in the Tibetan ecclesiastical system. He has local political power only in the region around Shigatse, 130 miles west of Lhasa, but the Chinese Communists enlarged his political power and used him as a counterweight to the Dalai Lama.

† Lower House of India's Parliament. The Upper House is known as Rajya Sabha (Council of States).

him that they had deliberately circulated false rumors to mislead the Chinese into thinking that the Dalai Lama would be coming to India by the Lhasa-Gyantse-Yatung-Gangtok trade route. As diversionary tactics they had cut off the Chinese communications between Yatung and Lhasa. Early in April Chinese troops appeared in this area and were subjected to continuous harassment by Khamba guerrillas. One trader told of seeing white soldiers, "tall, with blue eyes, light hair, wearing black boots and khaki trousers," in the vicinity of Gyantse on April 22nd. They were accompanied by women, also European, who "looked like nurses in white uniforms." They came in trucks and in a trailer attached to a jeep which was equipped with machine guns on top, and were given a warm welcome by the Chinese. Could they have been Russians? Or were they technicians with their wives?

The Chinese had made efforts to prevent the Dalai Lama leaving Tibet. Within a few hours of realizing that His Holiness had left Lhasa, they began a mammoth manhunt by air and land. Their land operations are reckoned to have involved some fifty thousand troops, and not long after the Dalai Lama's departure heavy artillery fire was heard south of Lhasa where the Chinese shelled rebels entrenched at Nethang, the royal party's rendezvous in the first stage of their flight from the capital. This rebel group comprised a rearguard party left behind to cover up the Dalai Lama's flight and to check pursuit. The Chinese air operations were equally painstaking and thorough. The area which the Dalai Lama's party were traversing after March 19th was over 350 miles wide and around 75 miles deep, stretching south of the Brahmaputra from Nagartse to Lho Dzong in the east, and inhabited, apart from the Khambas, by the equally rebellious and independent Amdo and Golok tribes. While the planes flew low over the valleys and towering peaks the troops combed villages and mountain monasteries in a desperate but vain attempt to intercept the Dalai Lama. In the twenty hours which elapsed between the God-king's crossing of the Tsangpo and the Chinese discovery that he had fled Lhasa, the royal party had covered over fifty miles. Mindol-ling lies thirty miles southeast of the Tsangpo, and twenty-five miles farther east is Tsetang. Persistent grilling of villagers and monks along the route north of the Tsangpo produced little of value to the Chinese, for the journey had been made under cover of night.

Nor were the aerial reconnaissances any more fruitful. Here two things hampered the Chinese. In their reckoning, the Dalai Lama would either stay in southwest Tibet, as he had done during the Han "liberation" of Tibet in 1950 when he had moved his temporary government to Yatung near the Indian border, or proceed to Bhutan or Sikkim. The Dalai Lama did neither. Another retrogressive factor affecting the Chinese was the weather. For the greater part of the eleven days which the royal party required to cover the hundred-odd miles from Tsetang to the Indian frontier, a thick wall of cloud hung over the eastern Himalayas, making visibility poor and hindering aerial pursuit. Under the blanket of cloud enfolding the mountaintops, the Dalai Lama slipped into India. It is curious but true that on the morning after the night of March 31st when the Dalai Lama entered India the clouds lifted and the sun shone brightly. Some Tibetan lamas have been known to claim occult powers which enable them to control the weather, inducing rain in a season of drought or sunshine when the clouds threaten a flood.

Whatever the cause, the fact is that the Dalai Lama's party after crossing the Brahmaputra sighted aircraft only twice— the first time on the fifth day out of Lhasa when in the vicinity of Tsetang, and the second time when approaching the Indian border. On the first occasion the Chinese plane, which passed at some distance, did not spot them; the second plane they believed to be Indian. Twice again they heard aircraft while south of the Brahmaputra, but were unable to see anything owing to the dense, unseasonable clouds. It is doubtful if the Chinese parachuted troops at any point along the Dalai Lama's route, for the simple reason that they never sighted him. Nor did the party at any time see Chinese troops or hear of them being in the vicinity.

From Tsetang the Living Buddha with his entourage moved up the mountains south through the Trigu Valley, traveling some forty miles to Trigu Lake in the heart of the Nyem area, the chief stronghold in rebel hands. The region is fairly populous, and enmeshed with caravan routes which thread their way through the mountains and the plain. Crowds gathered at every encampment where the Dalai Lama halted, and wherever he could give them a public audience and his blessing. It was imperative, however, that no time should be lost unnecessarily, and such halts and delays as were inevitable were reduced to the minimum.

Some fifty miles to the south of Trigu Lake is Tsona Dzong. While approaching this district, and while still two days' ride from the Chuthangmu Pass which leads into the Northeast Frontier Agency (NEFA), whose eight-hundred-mile frontier of mountainous terrain abuts on Tibet, the Dalai Lama dispatched two emissaries with a message requesting the Government of India to permit him and his party to enter India and to seek asylum there. The emissaries reached officials at the Indian checkpost of Chuthangmu on March 29th. They informed the Indian authorities that the God-king was expected to reach the border at Kanzey Mane near Chuthangmu in the Kameng Frontier Division of NEFA on March 30th. His route from Tsona Dzong to the Indian frontier ran for ten miles along the Towang Chu River. The Government of India, already apprised of the possibility of the Dalai Lama's seeking asylum in India, had, in

Mr. Nehru's words to Parliament, "instructed the checkposts round about there what to do in case such a development took place." On the evening of March 31st the God-king, accompanied by his mother, brother, sister, three cabinet ministers, and two tutors, was received by the assistant political officer of the Tawang subdivision, and crossed into Indian territory. He was followed shortly afterward by the remainder of his party. Dividing later into two groups, they proceeded to Tawang, the site of one of India's largest Buddhist monasteries, which is about forty miles down the valley, close to the eastern border of Bhutan.

Mr. Nehru disclosed the news of the Dalai Lama's entry into India in a statement to the Lok Sabha on April 3rd, but Hong Kong newspapers, quoting the official Chinese news agency report, had released the news the day before. Obviously the course of the Living Buddha's journey in the last stages of his three-hundred-mile trek was known to the Chinese, but by then he was beyond their reach. It must also have been known to their intelligence agents inside India, who are concentrated largely in Kalimpong, a hill station in the foothills of the Himalayas which teems with spies and counterspies of varied political hues. Indifferent communications in NEFA accounted for Mr. Nehru not receiving the Dalai Lama's message of March 29th until April 1st, for no direct wireless facilities exist between the border checkposts and New Delhi; messages have to be relayed by wireless from Bomdila, headquarters of the Kameng Frontier Division, to Shillong, capital of Assam State.

Once the Chinese realized that the God-king was heading for India, their tone and attitude to that country changed perceptibly. On March 31st, the day the Dalai Lama crossed into India, the Peking *People's Daily,* while referring to India as China's "great and friendly neighbor," pointedly warned against foreign intervention in the developments in Tibet,

which, it stressed, "are entirely internal affairs of China."
It underlined this by stating flatly that Kalimpong was being
used as "a commanding center of rebellion" against Tibet,
although only three days previously the Indian prime minister had categorically denied the charge. The circulation of
the Peking editorial by the Chinese Embassy in Delhi an-
gered the Lok Sabha, which was also indignant that the
National Council of the Indian Communist party had almost
simultaneously issued a statement supporting the charge.
Tempers ran high in Parliament, and were concentrated on
the Communist members, who were angrily shouted down.
Mr. Nehru, who was not present in the Lok Sabha that day,
sought to mollify the mood of the House on the following
day. But it was obvious that, aside from the Communists, the
other members were not in a mood to be appeased.

Nor were the Chinese. Since the Dalai Lama's flight Peking
had been insisting that the Living Buddha had been "abducted" by his "traitorous advisers," an interpretation which
Mr. Nehru unequivocally declared that he did not accept. "As
for the Dalai Lama himself," he remarked in a speech to the
Lok Sabha, "I imagine that he left Lhasa of his own free will.
I cannot conceive of the Dalai Lama being pushed about
by his own people. People revere the Dalai Lama so much
that it is difficult to believe that the great mass of Tibetans
are against him." This could hardly have been to the liking
of Peking, whose tone in the face of mounting public criticism and indignation in India stiffened visibly. India was now
accused of expansionist aims in Tibet, and "Indian expansionist elements" were charged by the New China News
Agency of having "inherited this shameful legacy from the
British." The NCNA went on to explain: "That is why the
members of this gang [of Tibetan rebels] were of a mind to
join with foreign forces from within our country, with their
faces turned to India and their backs to the motherland. See

how affectionate they are with each other, calling each other sweet names and reluctant to part!" Mr. Nehru in a dignified rejoinder dismissed the allegation, affirming that "India had no political or ulterior ambitions in Tibet." He also repudiated the Chinese charge that the Dalai Lama was being held in India under duress. "They [the Chinese]," he observed in a speech to Parliament on April 27th, "have used the language of cold war regardless of truth and propriety. . . . The charges made against India are so fantastic that I find it difficult to deal with them. . . . It is therefore a matter of the deepest regret and surprise to us that charges should be made which are both unbecoming and entirely void of substance."

When Mr. Nehru said this, nine days had elapsed since the Dalai Lama himself had made his first statement on Indian soil at Tezpur. It had taken the party eighteen days to cover the 220-odd miles from Chuthangmu across the Sela Pass by way of Tawang and Bomdila to the railhead of Tezpur, which they reached after an arduous journey on foot, by horse, jeep, and car. For security reasons the Indian authorities had originally planned not to release the news of the Living Buddha's arrival until he was safely ensconced at Tawang within the "inner circle" of the NEFA area. But the premature Chinese announcement of his arrival in India induced a hasty change of plans. A strong detachment of Assam riflemen was sent to the border checkpost to ensure the safety of His Holiness, who was urged to lose no time in leaving for Tawang. The Northeast Frontier Agency was sealed off, only accredited officials and the local population being allowed entry. Private traffic was banned in the foothills region of Assam State, and identity cards were rigorously checked. At Chuthangmu the Dalai Lama's bodyguard surrendered their arms to the Indian authorities, and the Assam riflemen became the Living Buddha's escort. It was not expected that the Chinese would pursue the God-king across the Indian border, but there was always danger from saboteurs and other terrorist elements.

The point where the Dalai Lama entered India consists of mountainous, generally snow-clad terrain, but in the early spring the Sela Pass is aglow with flowers. Inside the giant white-walled monastery at Tawang, some ten thousand feet up in the mountains, six hundred shaven-headed monks chanted prayers for the God-king's safe journey, lit candles, and planted "prayer flags" on the green hillside. At Thongleng, a village not far from Tawang, the party split into two groups, the larger traveling ahead of the smaller group, which comprised the Dalai Lama and his entourage. These included, besides cabinet minister and tutors, a lord chamberlain, three lord attendants—master of ceremonies, master of robes, and master of tea—an Incarnate Lama,* and one representative each from the monasteries of Sera and Drepung. On the afternoon of April 5th the Dalai Lama's party was seen wending its way up the steep path leading to the monastery. This was lined with Buddhists in ceremonial robes and saffron-clad monks chanting hymns. The Dalai Lama, though cheerful, looked tired. Contrary to earlier reports he was neither injured nor ill. For security reasons it was decided that the Living Buddha should not put up at the monastery as originally arranged, but in a separate residence ringed by a unit of the Assam Rifles.

On April 8th the Dalai Lama set out for Bomdila, sixty-two miles from Tawang, along a mule track which traversed difficult mountain passes and deep valleys, through Jang, where the party halted briefly, to Sengi Dzong, some sixteen miles

* An Incarnate Lama, also known as Tulku Lama, is believed by the Tibetans to be a reincarnation of a bodhisattva, i.e., a holy man who attains nirvana (boundless bliss) but renounces his right to it in order to be reborn for the benefit of his fellow creatures. There are about 1,000 Tulku Lamas in Tibet today.

away, a journey which entailed some arduous trekking and riding on mules or on small Bhutan ponies. Bomdila which stands about nine thousand feet above sea level, is the highest administrative center in India. Overlooking the mountains are three snow peaks. The country is picturesque, with dense forests interspersed with gay flora. For the comfort of the royal party the Indian authorities had set up tents and bamboo shelters at intervals along the route.

Waiting to receive the royal party at Bomdila was P. N. Menon, former Indian consul general at Lhasa, whom Mr. Nehru had specially sent to meet the God-king and who was later attacked by the Chinese as the man responsible for master-minding the Living Buddha's Tezpur statement. The Dalai Lama reached Bomdila on April 12th, the last lap of his journey being along a bridle path winding through forested hills. From Bomdila a jeep track runs some seventy miles to the foot of the hills, where just across the border is an Assam Rifles post known as Foothills, which controls the border separating NEFA from the State of Assam. About the time of the Dalai Lama's arrival at Bomdila, an official spokesman in Delhi announced that the God-king would ultimately reside in the hill station of Mussoorie, and it was later learned that his residence would be in a house put at his disposal by the well-known Indian industrialist G. D. Birla. It was also officially stated that Mr. Nehru would see the Dalai Lama on April 24th, when the prime minister would be visiting Mussoorie for the conference of the All-India Association of Travel Agents.

At Bomdila a convoy of about thirty jeeps awaited the arrival of the party, which rested at this post for two days. The Living Buddha was described by a Tibetan who saw him there as looking "big and shining, wearing a magenta robe with a knitted handkerchief on his head." On April 17th the party reached Khelong, ten miles from Foothills, where they proceeded after a night's rest to Foothills and from there through the Darrang district of Assam to Tezpur. About twenty miles from Foothills on the Assam side is Missamari, where arrangements were later made to set up a camp for the Tibetan refugees.

Over fifty foreign and Indian correspondents had gathered at Foothills, which the Dalai Lama reached on the morning of April 18th a little after 7:30 A.M. It had been drizzling intermittently, and a mist hung over the mountainside. Before leaving Bomdila the God-king had held his first conference with his advisers on Indian soil. It was attended by the three cabinet ministers who had accompanied him, a former general of the Tibetan army, and high officials and monk dignitaries. The Dalai Lama impressed on his party the need to be inspired by Buddhist ideals, and adjured them not to abuse the hospitality of India, the land of the Buddha's birth. At the conference a code of conduct for Tibetans in India was framed which generally discussed the outlines of the press statement which the Dalai Lama was expected to issue at Tezpur. To the correspondents assembled at Foothills the God-king made no statement, but he looked buoyant and cheerful, and the serene smile rarely left his face.

After a brief halt at Foothills, the Dalai Lama, who was now transferred to a limousine which carried the Indian and Tibetan flags, the latter hastily improvised with crayons, left for Tezpur, arriving there about two hours later. Shortly before his arrival at the Circuit House, where the correspondents had assembled, a statement by the God-king was read on his behalf, first in Tibetan by Rimshi Surkhang Lhawang Tobgey, an official in his party, and then in English by another official, Jigme Pangdatshang. Copies of the statement were distributed to the correspondents.

In Peking at this time the second Chinese National People's Congress was in session, and among the delegates was

the Panchen Lama, clad in a gold robe and seated near Chou
En-lai. On the day the Dalai Lama reached Tezpur and issued
his historic statement categorically denying that he was in
India "under duress," and challenging the Chinese accusation
that he had been "abducted" by the rebels, the Chinese prime
minister repeated these charges. "Although the Dalai Lama
has been abducted to India," said Chou, "we still hope he
will be able to free himself from the hold of the rebels and
return to the motherland." At Tezpur on the same day the
Dalai Lama's statement declared: "The Dalai Lama would
like to state categorically that he left Lhasa and Tibet and
came to India of his own free will and not under duress. It
was due to the loyalty and affectionate support of his people
that the Dalai Lama was able to find his way through a route
which is quite arduous."

Even this categorical statement was repudiated by Peking
in a desperate effort to "save face." Commenting on it, the
Panchen Lama insisted: "The statement issued in the name
of the Dalai Lama, which turns things upside down, is a sheer
distortion of the facts and a complete fabrication. It is obviously a result of coercion by the reactionaries, and certainly
not of the Dalai Lama's own will." Evidently the term "reactionaries" was intended to include the Dalai Lama's Indian
hosts. But Peking could not erase facts merely by contradictions and insinuations.

The Dalai Lama's statement of April 18th was notable for
some other significant declarations. It began with the flat
assertion that "the Tibetan people are different from the Han
people of China," and went on to say that "there has always
been a strong desire for independence on the part of the
Tibetan people. Throughout history this has been asserted
on numerous occasions." The statement then discussed the
Sino-Tibetan agreement of 1951 when "the suzerainty of
China was accepted, as there was no alternative left to the

Tibetans," and declared that the full autonomy which Tibet was promised in return had not been respected and recognized by the Chinese. "In fact," observed the Dalai Lama's statement, "after the occupation of Tibet by the Chinese armies, the Tibetan Government did not enjoy any measure of autonomy even in internal matters, and the Chinese Government exercised full powers in Tibetan affairs." The picture of a small nation struggling unceasingly but unsuccessfully to preserve its independence from its powerful and aggressive neighbor emerges clearly from this account.

The statement went on to reveal that "by the end of 1955 a struggle had started in the Kham Province, and this assumed serious proportions in 1956." By early February, 1956, "the relations of Tibetans with China became openly strained." There followed a brief description of the events which had finally compelled the Living Buddha's advisers to suggest that the God-king should leave Tibet. In expressing his gratitude to the Indian people and government "for their spontaneous and generous welcome, as well as for the asylum granted to him and to his followers," the Dalai Lama's statement referred to the ancient religious, cultural, and trade links between India and Tibet, and described India as "the land of enlightenment, having given birth to the Lord Buddha." There is noticeable even in the reference to India an implied desire that Tibet should be treated as equal and sovereign, and not as a humble suppliant dependent on India's benefactions.

It is also significant that the statement, while demanding freedom from China, implying either independence or real autonomy, did not shut the door on any solution—on negotiation, arbitration, or reference to the United Nations. But there could be no going back to Tibet's post-1951 status. The Dalai Lama concluded his statement, couched throughout in the third person, a fact to which the Chinese later were to attach a sinister significance, with the fervent hope that, "These troubles will be over soon without any more bloodshed. As Dalai Lama and spiritual head of all Buddhists in Tibet, his foremost concern is the well-being of his people and in ensuring the perpetual flourishing of his sacred religion and the freedom of his country." The emphasis the statement lays on the Dalai Lama's religious and secular functions and on the right to religious and political freedom flowing therefrom is interesting and revealing.

Confronted with this frank, forthright, and assertive document, the Chinese Communists reacted characteristically, mounting a barrage of vituperative denial and abuse which questioned the authenticity of the "so-called statement of the Dalai Lama," describing it as "a crude document, lame in reasoning, full of lies and loopholes." The Chinese dismissed the Tibetan claim to independence as contrary to historic facts, and insisted that Peking had controlled Tibet's political and religious systems from the thirteenth to the eighteenth centuries. "Not even the title, position and powers of the Dalai Lama were laid down by the Tibetans themselves," affirmed the New China News Agency. The Tibetans, it conceded, are different from the Hans, but so are the Mongolians, Manchus, Uighurs, Huis, Chuangs, Miaos, Yaos, and "dozens of other small nationalities in the southern provinces." None of these small nationalities had claimed independence, though they had enjoyed regional autonomy "within the big family of their motherland." The same NCNA commentator observed, with an implied innuendo on Indian involvement: "The publication at this time of this so-called statement of the Dalai Lama, which harps on so-called Tibetan independence, will naturally cause people to ask: Is this not an attempt to place the Dalai Lama in a position of hostility to his motherland and thus to block the road for him to return to it? Is this not an attempt to create a situation for compelling the Indian Government to permit the Tibetan rebels to engage in anti-Chinese political activities in India?" The rebels were, of course, denounced as "reactionaries," representative of vested interests who were opposed to the reforms and modernization schemes introduced by the Chinese Communists. The Panchen Lama again added his voice to this noisy chorus, particularly of critics of "Indian expansionism," and sarcastically referred to India's sudden solicitude for Buddhism, a religion it had successfully edged out of the country.

Meanwhile in India the Dalai Lama continued to receive the most friendly welcome by enthusiastic crowds along the rail route from Tezpur to Mussoorie. He left Tezpur in an air-conditioned coach at noon on Saturday, April 18th, after receiving an address of welcome from the citizens of Tezpur and giving his blessings to them in the traditional Buddhist way. On Sunday morning the special train halted at Siliguri in West Bengal for nearly seventy-five minutes, and there a mammoth crowd, estimated at several thousands, greeted him. They included the children of the Dalai Lama's elder brother, who had come from their school in Darjeeling to greet him. Also there to pay the God-king his respects was the Maharajkumar of Sikkim with members of his family. Waiting to welcome him were monks bearing wooden incense burners, some with long trumpets and other musical instruments with which they greeted the God-king. The crowds shouted, "Down with Chinese imperialism!" As the Dalai Lama stepped onto the rostrum which had been erected before the station, hundreds of Tibetans, men, women, and children, showered the traditional white scarves at him. A request for yellow flowers for his daily devotional prayers had been transmitted to Siliguri, and a large posy of saffron and yellow dahlias awaited the God-king when he alighted. The open space before the station presented a color-

ful scene with the thousands of Tibetans in flamboyant cos-
tumes of magenta, claret, pink, and purple. His Holiness
looked wan but cheerful.

On the way to Siliguri crowds had gathered by the wayside
stations in the hope of getting a glimpse of the God-king. The
train had halted at some points, and at the first stop on Saturday evening at Rangapara in Assam a large crowd broke
through the police cordon and gathered around the Dalai
Lama's coach. Farther on, at a small wayside station, Rangiya,
through which the train passed late at night, a crowd of a
few hundred villagers waited in the pouring rain merely to
see the train go by. These scenes were repeated throughout
the night as the heavily guarded royal coach moved toward
Siliguri. Early in the morning the train stopped at Bonarhat,
where among the crowd were some European planters from
the tea estates in the vicinity.

From Siliguri the train moved into the State of Bihar, an
area hallowed by Buddhism, for in Bihar Gautama centuries
ago had become the Buddha. Chapra was the last station in
Bihar, and there the Dalai Lama's train halted at 2:00 A.M.
amidst a huge crowd waving banners and shouting slogans,
greeting the God-king, who at that late hour was resting.
Shortly afterward the train crossed the frontier of Bihar into
Uttar Pradesh, which is Nehru's home state.

At Sarnath, where the Buddha had preached his dharma,
or eightfold way of life, the Dalai Lama alighted later that
morning on a platform festooned with flags and banners in a
station constructed on the lines of Buddhist architecture.
Along with the Tibetan monks were others from Ceylon,
Burma, Thailand, Cambodia, Vietnam, and India. The Dalai
Lama, accompanied by this colorful retinue, proceeded to
the Dhamek Stupa, reputedly built by India's great apostle-
emperor Asoka, a convert to Buddhism, where the God-king
knelt in prayer. He also offered a silk scarf to the golden

image of the Buddha in the Mulganda Kuti Vihara, whose great bell, tolled only for highly distinguished visitors, chimed throughout the morning in the Living Buddha's honor.

At Banaras, the Rome of Hinduism, the Dalai Lama's party changed into a broad-gauged train for Dehra Dun, and arrived there early in the morning of April 21st. A crowd of over three thousand awaited His Holiness, and in a long motorcade he drove to Birla House at Mussoorie, which was his journey's end, some 1,500 miles from Lhasa. It was a little over a month since the God-king had left his capital. At Gandhi Chowk, the center of Mussoorie, the Dalai Lama was welcomed with flowers by the chairman of the local municipal board.

What was his status to be in India? On April 20th, a day before His Holiness arrived at Mussoorie, questions were asked in the Lok Sabha at Delhi to which initially Nehru gave equivocal replies. The Dalai Lama, said India's prime minister, would be free to carry on his religious activities in India, "but political activities are not carried on from one country against another." When a veteran Independent member, the highly respected Dr. H. N. Kunzru, pointed out that in Britain, when asylum was granted, refugees were allowed to carry on normal propaganda in favor of their views but were prohibited from collecting arms or making warlike preparations, Mr. Nehru observed that it was difficult to draw the line. It would be permitted to one to some extent but not to another. In reply to other questions the prime minister said that the Dalai Lama was a responsible person acting in a responsible way but that there were many others and that "we do not know how they might function." It was, continued Mr. Nehru, the ordinary right of any country, including Britain, to limit the function of foreigners who created difficulties with other countries. The rule of law was that a country had the right to limit such activities—to what extent and in what manner was a matter of circumstances and situation.

The Indian prime minister's replies and elucidation are interesting in view of subsequent developments, and might conceivably affect and influence future events. On April 24th Mr. Nehru met the Dalai Lama, whom he had last seen some three years before. As the prime minister remarked to a group of newspapermen shortly after his four-hour talk with the God-king: "He does not come to us as a vague, mystical figure. He comes here as one we know." Mr. Nehru revealed that the Dalai Lama had admitted writing the letters to General Tan Kuan-san but said that the God-king "was then passing through highly troubled times." He had had, he said, "a fairly good talk and I hope a helpful talk with the Dalai Lama." Had it not been that the prime minister had another engagement, he might have continued the discussion for another hour or so. India's interest in Tibet, Mr. Nehru stressed, was "historical, sentimental and religious, and not essentially political." Of course, he himself would try for a peaceful solution of the Tibetan problem, and he would welcome the Panchen Lama "or anyone else . . . the Chinese ambassador or any Chinese emissary," who might want to meet the Dalai Lama. Mr. Nehru hoped that subsequently conditions would be created for the return of the God-king to Tibet but said that "this as well as other things should not be the subject of heated exchanges and debate." The prime minister observed that his government was anxious "not to muzzle" the Dalai Lama but that at the same time "we do expect him to keep in view the difficulties of the situation and speak or act accordingly." He revealed that when the Dalai Lama visited India in 1956 the God-king had told him that Tibet was spiritually advanced but socially and economically backward. His Holiness had repeated the statement in his talk that day. Mr. Nehru suggested that the Dalai Lama "has more anxiety for conditions in Tibet, in a peaceful solution, and not in giving press interviews." It was an oblique but obvious hint to the God-king.

Nonetheless, about two months later, on June 20th, the Dalai Lama chose to receive press correspondents at Mussoorie and to circulate a two-thousand-word statement which went specifically and categorically far beyond his Tezpur statement. Nothing short of the pre-1950 status of Tibet, he flatly declared, would be acceptable to him, and this would be a condition precedent to the reopening of negotiations with the Chinese, wherein he would welcome a foreign mediator. "We ask for peace and for a peaceful settlement," he declared. "But we must also ask for the maintenance of the status and rights of our state and people." The Sino-Tibetan agreement of 1951 had been concluded as "between two independent and sovereign states." At the same time the Dalai Lama accused the Chinese of obtaining the agreement under duress, and charged them with forging the Tibetan seal affixed to the document. "Wherever I am," he declared in answering a question, "the Tibetan people will recognize me as the Government of Tibet." Indeed, the Dalai Lama's statement, with its frequent reiteration of the phrase "I and my Government," read like the pronouncement of an *émigré* government.

His Holiness charged the Chinese not only with obstructing reforms which his own government sought to introduce in Tibet but also of instituting a reign of terror. They had, he alleged, introduced forced labor, indulged in compulsory exactions, persecuted the people, and plundered and confiscated property belonging to individuals and the monasteries. Thousands of Tibetans had been imprisoned and hundreds executed. The Dalai Lama stated that he would welcome an investigation into these charges by an international commission. "I and my Government," he declared, "will readily abide by the verdict of such an impartial body." His Holiness also disclosed, though this was widely known, that during his last visit to India he had told Mr. Nehru that he was unwilling to return to Tibet "until there was a manifest change in the attitude of the Chinese authorities," and had sought the Indian prime minister's advice. At that time Chou En-lai was also in India; and Nehru, after consulting him, and on receiving assurances that China would respect her undertakings with Tibet, had advised the Dalai Lama to return. His Holiness was asked whether the Chinese would gain or lose by his being in exile.

"The Chinese should be able to answer that question," said the God-king with a seraphic smile.

He estimated that since 1956 the number of Tibetans killed while fighting the Chinese forces exceeded the figure of 65,000 given in a report filed before the International Commission of Jurists. What the Chinese aimed to do, said His Holiness, was to exterminate Buddhist religion and culture in Tibet and to absorb the Tibetan people.

Would he appeal for arms on behalf of the rebel patriots who, according to him, were still fighting in eastern and northern Tibet?

"Although," said the Dalai Lama, "I have no intention to leave the National Volunteer Defense Army unaided, I am intending to help them by all means of a peaceful solution rather than by military force."

It was an answer as skillful as any Nehru might have given in similar circumstances. The God-king seemed well aware that he had no effective sanctions behind him except the moral conscience and indignation of the civilized world, and to that also he appealed—"to the conscience of all peace-loving and civilized nations," as he put it.

But would the civilized world respond to his appeal? Tibet was even more mysterious and remote than Czechoslovakia had seemed two decades earlier.

roof
of
the
world

CHAPTER TWO

"Where is your God?" A Chinese Communist once sarcastically demanded of a Tibetan. "You are born. You die."

"He is everywhere," said the Tibetan simply.

The Chinese filled a bowl with water and, tilting it, poured the water onto the ground between them.

"Like this water," he said somberly, "you too will go down into the earth. Where is your God?"

Tibet, land of lamas,* is inevitably a land of religion. Since at least one son from each family is expected to become a monk, it is estimated that about one-quarter of all Tibetan males enter the priesthood. Lhasa's "Big Three" monasteries —Drepung (Rice Heap), Sera (Rose Fence), and Ganden

---

* A lama is a senior monk who has studied the Tibetan scriptures closely, done religious penance, and practiced meditation. Junior monks are known as *dabas* or *trapas*.

32

(Joyous)—are said to house between them some 20,000 inmates, almost half the population of the capital city. In the whole of Tibet there are believed to be over 300,000 monks attached to the numerous monasteries scattered over the country, as well as many thousands of nuns. From childhood every Tibetan is taught to pray in the shrine room of his house, and most Tibetans carry their 108-bead rosaries and their prayer wheels, which are called *korlos*.

Since the Dalai Lama sought asylum in India nearly twelve thousand Tibetan refugees are believed to have entered the country. Their reason for leaving is mainly Chinese efforts to exterminate their religion and to absorb them. More than any other coercive measures of the Han intruders, this has deeply affected the lives of the common people. "They started talking very nicely and sweetly," said a Tibetan refugee. "But later on they troubled us quite a bit."

The Tibetans, a cheerful, friendly people, have always been sturdily independent. Geography and history have conspired to encourage this outlook. Until the Communist aggression of 1950 Tibet was one of the most isolated and impenetrable countries in the world. It covers a vast plateau in Central Asia, in area about 500,000 square miles, bounded on the north by Sinkiang, or Chinese Turkestan, on the south by Nepal, Bhutan, and Sikkim, along with 800 miles of mountainous Indian territory; on the west by the Ladakh area of Kashmir, and on the east by China. Tibet's terrain is around 10,000 feet above sea level; but large areas in the north are over 16,000 feet in elevation, with mountains alternating with plains and valleys, the so-called northern plains being known as the Chang Tang. It is bitterly cold there and the area is desolate, inhabited for the most part by hardy nomadic tribes. Southern Tibet, which contains Lhasa, the capital, and which also encompasses the valleys of the Tsangpo, the Indus, and the Sutlej rivers, really forms Tibet proper, with the two important towns of Shigatse and Gyantse. Western, or Upper, Tibet has three districts, including the gold mines of Jalung, to which Herodotus referred in somewhat mythical terms. Along the eastern border, on both sides of the Sino-Tibetan frontier, reside the warlike Khambas and the Goloks, with the Amdos just across the northeast border. A large part of the population in the Chinese districts abutting Tibet's northern and eastern frontiers is Tibetan. These districts include Chinghai and Szechwan, and Yunnan in the south. Many mountain ranges run across the plateau in a west-east direction, the most important being the Tangla Range, which is an extension of the Karakoram. Eastern Tibet, also known as the Land of the Great Corrosions, is crisscrossed with canyons and high mountains, particularly in the region around Chamdo, which is inhabited by the Khambas. Through this area run the Yangtse, Mekong, Salween, and Irrawady rivers with their tributaries.

The Tibetans call their country Bhot, a term widely used in India, where the inhabitants of Tibet are called Bhotias. Probably the word Tibet is a European adaptation of To-bhot, or High Bhot, the name by which the great plateau with its uplands bordering the frontiers of China, Mongolia, and Kashmir is known to Tibetans. The term "Tibet" first occurs about A.D. 950 in the works of the Arab writer Istakhri, who calls the country "Tobbat."

Since no official census has been taken in Tibet except by the Chinese Communists, whose statistics are somewhat resilient, it is not possible to estimate the population accurately. Their number is probably in the neighborhood of two million in Tibet with around another two million outside its frontiers. Moreover the spiritual authority of the Dalai Lama is not confined to Tibet alone, but extends to Ladakh, Sikkim, Bhutan, Sinkiang, the Buriat-Mongolian Republic of the Soviet Union, and the Kalmucks, who inhabit a region northwest of the Caspian Sea and south of the Volga.

Landlocked by geography, Tibet has also historically remained the Hidden Land. Of its history prior to the seventh
century after Christ little is known, its real history beginning
with the reign of the great Song-tsan Gampo who ruled Tibet
from A.D. 620 to 650. He introduced an alphabet, formulated
a code of criminal law and a code of morals, and conquered
Upper Burma and western China, subjecting the Chinese to a
humiliating treaty which entailed giving the Tibetan king a
Chinese princess in marriage. Her name was Wen-Cheng, and
equally lovely and intelligent was the king's other wife, Princess Bhrukuti-Devi, daughter of the king of Nepal. Both the
queens were devout Buddhists, and although Buddhism had
entered Tibet about two hundred years earlier the queens
persuaded the king to restore the influence of that religion,
whose power had waned. It was Song-tsan Gampo who laid
the foundations of the Potala and made Lhasa his capital.

In the second half of the eighth century, a Tantric * teacher
from India, Padma Sambhava, known as Guru Rimpoche
(the precious teacher), was summoned to the court of King
Ti-Song Detsan, grandson of Song-tsan Gampo. The strength
of Buddhism had flagged again, and Guru Rimpoche was
successful in reviving it by adapting Buddhism to the earliest
form of worship in Tibet, known as Bon. This was a mixture
of Shamanism or nature worship, divination, the exorcising
of devils, propitiation of various spirits, and animal sacrifice.
Devil worship was a prominent feature of this primitive cult.
By incorporating many Bon beliefs and practices into the
Buddhist ritual, Guru Rimpoche evolved Lamaism, which
is the religion of Tibet. It includes a widespread belief in
reincarnation. We shall have occasion to examine its development and sects in greater detail later.

During the reign of Ti-Song Detsan, China paid a yearly
tribute of 50,000 yards of Chinese brocade to Tibet. This was
in the era of the glorious T'ang dynasty which ruled China

* Tantricism is the worship of the divine energy (*Shakti*) in a female form.

from A.D. 618 to 907 and gave that country a strong centralized administration. In A.D. 763 the Tibetans invaded the
border regions of China in great strength and sacked the city
of Chang An. During the second half of the eighth century
and the first half of the ninth, the Tibetans continued their
encroachments upon Chinese territory, acquiring most of
western Kansu and large parts of western Szechwan, and it
was only around A.D. 850, when internal rivalries sapped the
strength of Tibet's ruling dynasty, that the Chinese were able
to hold the Tibetans in check.

In the eleventh century the long line of Tibetan kings
came to an end with the death of Lang Darma, and interne-
cine warfare reduced Tibet from a monarchy to a congeries
of small principalities ruled by petty chieftains. In this
political chaos the religious strength of Lamaism began to
assert itself, and by the end of the eleventh century the new
religion took strong root throughout the country. Lamaism
received a tremendous impetus in the second half of the
thirteenth century when the hierarchy of the Sakya lamas,
taking their name from the monastery at Sakya in Central
Tibet, obtained political recognition from the Mongol emperor of China, Kublai Khan, who embraced Lamaism and
gave the sovereignty of Tibet to the high priest of the Sakya
lamas. This dynasty of priest-kings ruled for some seventy
years until 1345, when twenty successive Sakya lamas had
administered the country.

Genghiz Khan, who laid the fortunes of the Mongols, descended on China in 1210, capturing Peking but leaving the
task of conquering the rest of the country to his generals while
he turned to western Asia. The accession of Kublai Khan and
the foundation of a new capital at Peking in 1263 mark the
establishment of a separate Mongol Empire. Historically the
reign of the Mongol Yuan dynasty begins in 1279 when the
last of the Sung pretenders was destroyed and Kublai Khan's

domains covered all China and Tibet. The Mongol Empire, based on terror, remained peaceful only as long as its rulers were strong. Kublai Khan's death in 1294 saw the decline of his dynasty, which was replaced by the Mings in China in 1368. The Mings made way for the Manchus in 1644.

During the Ming period, and indeed for some years before that, Tibet functioned as a virtually independent kingdom. The Mings were more interested in extending their authority northward than in ensuring stability in the south. Some fifty years after Kublai Khan's death the Sakya priest-kings whom he had entrenched in sovereignty over Tibet were replaced by the Sitya dynasty, who continued to rule until 1635, and successfully asserted their independence vis-à-vis China. In the second half of the seventeenth century Tibet was blessed by the rule of a remarkable Dalai Lama, Lobsang Gyatse, known as "The Great Fifth," * who journeyed to Peking, where he was acknowledged by the then Manchu emperor of China as an independent sovereign. Lobsang Gyatse, a strong and farsighted ruler, rebuilt the Potala, much of which the Mongols had destroyed. He was able to control the Mongols who were concentrated in Yunnan, which was one reason why the Manchus, who were troubled by them, cultivated his good will. During his lifetime the first European, a Portuguese named Antonio de Andrada, entered Tibet, but did not reach Lhasa or Shigatse.

The sixth Dalai Lama, Tsang-Yang Gyatse, a talented poet but a man of dissolute habits, was murdered in eastern Tibet by the Chinese in 1706. There was trouble in Tibet following the installation of the seventh Dalai Lama, Lobsang Kesang Gyatse, and the Manchus took advantage of the dissensions to dispatch a military expedition to Lhasa in 1720. Tibet was compelled to recognize Chinese sovereignty in 1727, and a system of diplomatic relations was established whereunder a

* He was the fifth Dalai Lama.

Chinese *amban,* or representative, was stationed at Lhasa. The number of ambans was later raised to two, and they interfered in Tibetan administration. In 1750, resenting the interference of the ambans, who had put the Tibetan regent to death, the Tibetans in turn massacred the Chinese in Lhasa, but Peking's authority was soon reestablished by an army dispatched by the emperor of China. Significantly, this period of Tibetan subservience coincides with the apex of the Manchu dynasty under the emperors Yung Cheng and Chien Lung. Following the example of the Emperor Kang Hsi who preceded them, they extended the boundaries of the Chinese Empire, subduing not only Tibet but also conquering Mongolia and Turkestan.

In the eighteenth and nineteenth centuries Tibet was virtually a vassal of the Celestial Empire, which through its ambans at Lhasa supervised the nomination of every new Dalai Lama. In 1893 the thirteenth Dalai Lama, Tupten Gyatse, who was born in 1876, assumed temporal power, holding it through various vicissitudes until his death in 1933. He succeeded in 1911 in getting rid of the Chinese who had forced him to flee to India a year earlier. It was not his first exile. At the time that the Younghusband expedition * had moved on Lhasa in 1904, the Dalai Lama took refuge in Mongolia, returning to Tibet five years later. By steering skillfully between the Chinese, the British, and the Russians he was able eventually to restore *de facto* independence to his country.

The Mongols were no more Han than are the Tibetans. Nor were the Manchus, who, like the Mongols, also intermittently attempted in later years to assert their sovereignty over Tibet. Though Tibet's relations with China go back to

* This expedition, led by Sir Francis Younghusband, was launched in 1904 during Lord Curzon's viceroyalty in India, and was actuated by British suspicions that the Dalai Lama was allegedly plotting with the Russians to keep the British out of Tibet.

the seventh century, their character has never remained constant but has varied with the strength of China's central government. Thus, taking advantage of geography to influence history, the Tibetans have asserted their independence when the Chinese were weak and unwillingly accepted Peking's authority when the Chinese were overwhelmingly strong. This has been so even up to the eve of the Dalai Lama's flight from Lhasa in March, 1959.

The contention, therefore, that in assessing Tibet's political status only the views of China should be taken into account is manifestly unfair to the Tibetans, whose own point of view cannot be brusquely brushed aside. For considerable stretches of their history—the last, for forty years from 1911 to 1951—they have remained aloof from the Chinese claim to overlordship and have functioned as an independent government. Even in negotiating the Lhasa Convention in 1904, following the Younghusband expedition, the British Government dealt directly with Tibet, thereby impliedly recognizing its special status, although the Chinese Imperial Resident was allowed to "examine" the treaty before the signatures were appended. In fact Britain claimed and was accorded recognition as the most-favored nation with "special interests" in Tibet.

By Article 9 of the Convention, Tibet agreed not to send out representatives abroad or to permit any foreign power to intervene in its affairs without the previous consent of the British. Thus China, though nominally consulted, was really excluded. By the Peking Convention of 1906 China confirmed the Lhasa Convention, with some minor modifications affecting customs dues and the establishment of trading stations, but also secured one major point from Britain—that the preservation of Tibet's integrity should be China's responsibility and that China alone should have the right to concessions in Tibet. The Tibetans greatly resented their exclusion from the conference in Peking. The term "suzerain" as governing the relations between China and Tibet was first used in the St. Petersburg Convention of 1907 when Russia also recognized Britain's "special interest" in the maintenance of the *status quo* in the external relations of Tibet, but both Powers agreed to enter into negotiations with Tibet only through the intermediary of China, "except on matters arising out of the Lhasa Convention." Britain thereby secured what she had set out to achieve—to keep Russia out of Tibet, which henceforth would serve as a buffer between India (then under British rule) and China. The price for this was the recognition of Chinese "suzerainty" while simultaneously acknowledging Tibet's autonomy. Yet this fiction of suzerainty soon wore thin, as Britain demonstrated in 1914 when she invited China and Tibet to a tripartite conference with herself at Simla, Tibetan plenipotentiaries taking part in the discussions on an equal footing with the British and Chinese delegates.

At Simla the Tibetans on British persuasion agreed to accept a treaty by which the Chinese were accorded the right to maintain a mission in Lhasa, though they were strictly forbidden to interfere in the internal affairs of Tibet. In 1911, after the decrepit Manchu Empire had collapsed, the Tibetans expelled the Chinese forces, and the Dalai Lama declared Tibet independent. China's first Republican president, Yuan Shih-kai, proclaimed Tibet to be an integral part of China, but he was unsuccessful when he attempted to implement his declaration by military force. The Simla Convention, held on British initiative, followed this attempt.

Although the Chinese plenipotentiaries had agreed to the terms of the Convention, Peking refused to ratify them, thereby releasing the Tibetans from their undertaking to acknowledge Chinese suzerainty. From then until the Sino-Tibetan agreement of May, 1951, following the first Com-

munist aggression designed to "liberate" Tibet, that country
functioned for all practical purposes as independent until
again—this time under the guns of the Communist Chinese
—she was forced to recognize "the unified leadership of the
Central People's Government," but did so only on Peking's
pledge that "the Tibetan people have the right of exercising
national regional sovereignty." More specifically, the Communists undertook not to alter the existing political system in
Tibet or the established status, functions, and powers of the
Dalai Lama, and to respect the religious beliefs, customs,
and habits of the Tibetan people. Additionally they promised that "in matters related to various reforms in Tibet,
there will be no compulsion on the part of the central authorities."

The Chinese violated every one of these pledges. Even as
in 1914 repudiation by Peking of the Simla Convention released the Tibetans of their undertaking to recognize Chinese
suzerainty, the violation by Peking of its pledges under the
Sino-Tibetan agreement of 1951 permitted Lhasa to denounce the agreement and proclaim Tibet's independence.
In international as in private agreements all the parties concerned must fulfill their undertakings if their contracts are
to be valid and enforceable.

What sort of people are the Tibetans? Most of what is
known of them prior to the seventh century of the Christian
era is based on myth and legend. According to Tibetan tradition the human race was born in Tibet and originated from
the marriage of a monkey with an ogress. Indians identify
the monkey with Hanuman, the monkey-god of the Hindu
pantheon, who was a protégé of Avalokiteshwara, the Lord
of Mercy, whom the Tibetans call Chen-re-si, the Compassionate Spirit. Tibetan legend holds that the Compassionate
Spirit entered into the body of the monkey. Thus the Tibetans trace their descent from Chen-re-si, who permitted

Hanuman to marry the mountain ogress. From their saintly paternal ancestor the Tibetans claim the virtues of piety, fortitude, charity, and diligence, while their deficiencies, such as greed, lust, love for trade, obstinacy, and bad temper they attribute to their female progenitor.

Whatever the legend, the likely fact is that Tibet's people, like its plants, have a postglacial origin, being immigrants from the steppes and deserts farther to the north when Tibet, which apparently was once an ice desert, became habitable. In appearance they vary greatly, although the Mongoloid strain is pronounced. Some might be taken for Annamese or even for Persians or Navajo Indians. Their complexions range from pink, generally among the children, to brown. By temperament they are rugged and gay, smile spontaneously, and have a simplicity of manner which places them among the most natural people in the world.

Before the Communist invasion Tibet's people fell broadly into four classes—nobles, traders, peasants, and nomads. The nobility, which owned most of the country's land and wealth, formed a class apart and traced its descent from one of three sources. The oldest and smallest section of the aristocracy comprised descendants of the early monarchs who ruled Tibet before the tenth century of the Christian era. The second were descendants of the families in which a Dalai Lama or a Panchen Lama was born, for these families were automatically ennobled and given large estates by the government. The third section was composed of individuals whose ancestors had rendered meritorious service to the country and were duly rewarded. Certain peculiar customs relating to property prevailed among the nobility. Although property generally descended from father to sons, it was bestowed on the daughter where there were no sons, and when she married she adopted her husband into the family. This meant that she did not change her name but that the husband took hers.

The name by which the family of an existing Dalai Lama is known is Yap-shi Sar-pa, which means the New Patrimony. But the moment the Dalai Lama dies, or in the Tibetan phrase "retires to the heavenly fields," his family changes its name.

Traders in Tibet constitute what might be called the middle class, though there has never been a real middle class in the country. But they rank intermediately between the landed gentry and the peasants. Though simple, the Tibetans are by no means artless, and have a strong commercial sense. Besides the professional traders, nobles and monks also engage in trade. Tibetan women are free from seclusion, and many of them manage shops and engage in small retail business while their menfolk take charge of the commercial dealings which necessitate long and often arduous journeys.

Tibet does not lack arable land, but most of it is underdeveloped owing to want of manpower because large numbers of the male population take to a monastic life which ordains celibacy, which in turn controls the birth rate. The position of peasants vis-à-vis their landlords has been virtually that of serfs, for no peasant is allowed to quit his land without the landlord's permission. This is rarely given, and then only for a monetary compensation. Though slavery is not common in Tibet, slaves exist; and, oddly enough, they are often treated better than the paid servants or tenants. They are also allowed to move freely, and theatrical troupes that tour Tibet are mainly drawn from the menial classes.

In the fourth class fall the shepherds and herdsmen, the nomads who work largely in the uplands, descending once a year to lower levels to sell their produce of wool, salt, yak tails, and butter, and in return to purchase commodities not available in the uplands, such as barley, wheat, tea, and woolen clothes. This grazier class is known for its hardihood and independence.

Women enjoy a remarkably high status, and in an older day, when Tibet was split into principalities, the chieftain was often—and sometimes still is—a woman. Like the women of Burma, the women of Tibet are influential not only in home affairs but also in business and, where their husbands are officials, in affairs of state. The only realm in which their position might be described as inferior is the religious domain, where, significantly, of the three forms of blessings accorded by the Dalai Lama the lowest is reserved for all women except one. The exception is Dor-je Pa-mo, the only female incarnation in Tibet, who is the head of a monastery with male monk inmates at Sam-ding on Yamdrok Lake. Her name is interpreted as "Thunderbolt Sow," based on the Tibetan belief that she can change into that animal at will. Her predecessor, Pal-den Lha Mo ("The Glorious Goddess"), was also known in Sanskrit as "The Adamantine Whore." This female divinity is known as one of the "Eight Terrible Ones" and is depicted as riding on a white mule through a sea of blood. She is venerated as a special protector of the Dalai Lama and the Panchen Lama.

Marriage in Tibet is generally an arranged affair, a son being consulted by his father on the suitability of a bride chosen for him, while a daughter's opinion on her future husband is rarely, if at all, canvassed. Monogamy, polygamy, and polyandry are all practiced in Tibet, monogamy being the normal type of marriage. If a man is affluent, he may, if he so desires, indulge in polygamy, while at the other end of the economic ladder polyandry might be more convenient. In polyandry, practiced largely among the nomadic herdsmen and farmers, the wife is shared by her husband and his younger brothers but not by any elder.

Because Tibet is a theocratic state, its ruler, both civil and ecclesiastical, is the Dalai Lama, who theoretically enjoyed

absolute powers until the Chinese Communists whittled
down his authority, which depended largely on his personality and prestige. He appointed and dismissed officials, and
his judgment was invoked in all important cases, civil, criminal, and administrative. Custom decreed that all questions
requiring his decision should be put into writing and ten-
dered to His Holiness. Against each question was written the
sentence "To be or not to be," and the Dalai Lama signified
his command by placing a dot of bright blue ink, which no
other person is permitted to use, over whichever of the two
phrases he desired.

The first Dalai Lama was Ge-dun Truppa, who founded
the monastery at Tashi-lhunpo in the fifteenth century. Two
hundred years later it became the residence of the Panchen
Lama, a creation of the fifth Dalai Lama. Ge-dun Truppa
was a nephew of the great Lama Tsong Ka-pa (The Man
from the Land of Onions), who reorganized Lamaism late in
the fourteenth century and established the Gelugpa (The
Virtuous Way) sect, whose members were known as Yellow
Hats from the color of their headgear. Tsong Ka-pa also
founded the monasteries of Ganden and Sera. He might be
described as the Luther of Tibet. Earlier the dominant sect
was the Kadampa, or Ngingmapa, which was established by
an Indian pundit, Atisha, who came from Bengal to Tibet
in the opening years of the eleventh century. Members of
this sect wore red hats, and were known as such. Monks of
that order had been permitted to marry and drink, and they
soon became notorious for their lax living. The Yellow Hats
set out to reform Lamaism, and their monks were required
to observe celibacy, refrain from intoxicants, and to follow
a strict code of morals. Both the Dalai and the Panchen Lama
are members of the Gelugpa sect.

Ge-dun Truppa died in 1474, but his spirit was supposed
to have entered the body of a baby boy born two years later.

This child became his successor, and thus there came into being the system of priestly incarnation, the reincarnated being
known as Incarnate Lamas. The Dalai Lama was the first and
greatest of these, but the Tibetans acknowledge reincarnation in other lamas, who now number about a thousand. Two
of the present Dalai Lama's brothers, one of them older than
he, are held to be Incarnate Lamas. The elder one was proclaimed as such even before the discovery of the Dalai Lama.

In Tibet the Dalai Lama is known as Gyalpo Rimpoche
(Great Gem of Majesty). The title of Dalai Lama, which
means Ocean of Wisdom or Ocean Wide, was conferred on
the third Incarnate Lama, Sonam Gyatse, who as the third
Grand Lama of the Gelugpa sect converted a Mongol chieftain, Altan Khan, and spread the new faith to Mongolia. Like
Kublai Khan before him, Altan Khan sought to reward his
religious benefactor—not by bestowing a kingdom on him
but by investing him with a title. This happened in 1517.

The temporal overlordship of all Tibet was conferred
some years later, in 1640, on Lobsang Gyatse, the "Great
Fifth," who, allying himself with the Mongols, subdued the
lords of Tsang, a province at the gates of Lhasa. These
chieftains had disputed the power of the Gelugpa sect. In
return the Mongol Prince Gusri Khan conferred on the Great
Fifth the sovereignty of Tibet. Lobsang Gyatse also assumed
divinity, claiming to be the incarnation of Chen-re-si.

The procedure governing the search for and discovery of
the new Dalai Lama on the death of his predecessor is complicated and often protracted. Those responsible for the
choice are the heads of the three great monasteries of Drepung, Sera, and Ganden who are assisted by the state oracle
at the Nechung monastery near Lhasa and the oracle at
Samye, Tibet's oldest monastery. The search is generally instituted about three or four years after the Dalai Lama's
death, though the interval is sometimes longer. According

to Lamaist belief the soul of the dead Dalai Lama goes to dwell for forty-nine days in Lake Cho Kor Gye in southern Tibet before taking up residence in a newborn infant. The theory underlying this belief is that Tibet is ruled not by different Dalai Lamas but by successive appearances among mankind of the same spiritual entity, the bodhisattva Chen-re-si, who is known in India as Avalokiteshwara, the embodiment of compassion and benevolence. In the Lamaist pantheon the most important gods are the Buddha, Avalokiteshwara, and Amitabha, "the Boundless Light," whose reincarnation is held to be the Panchen Lama.

Sometimes one of the two oracles goes into a trance and is able to indicate where the new Dalai Lama lives. In the case of the present Dalai Lama, the oracle of Samye, after going into a trance, following a fruitless four-year search, advised that the investigation should be extended to the Chinese province of Chinghai, whose Amdo region is largely populated by Tibetans. Incidentally the great Tsong Ka-pa was born in Amdo. Here, along the shores of Lake Koko Nor, the fourteenth Dalai Lama, child of a humble peasant family, was discovered.

Before the child is accepted as the Living Buddha he is put through various tests. Some of his predecessor's possessions, such as his rosaries, liturgical drums and bells, handkerchiefs and teacups, are mixed with those belonging to other individuals, and the child is required to identify them. He is also examined for physical "signs of distinction." These include large ears, outstanding shoulders, "tiger-skin" spots on the legs, an imprint like a conch shell on one of the palms, and curving eyebrows. Normally he is invested with full authority on attaining eighteen, but until then a regent, assisted by a council of ministers, rules in his name.

The present Dalai Lama, whose name at birth was Lhamo Dhondup, later elongated to Jetsun Jampal Ngawang Lob-

sang Yishey Tenzing Gyatso Sisunwangyur Tshunpa Getson
Mapal Dhepal Sango, together with a litany of titles—Gentle
Glory, Mighty in Speech, Pure in Mind, of Absolute Wisdom,
Holder of the Dharma, Ocean Wide—was born on June 6,
1935, eighteen months after the death of the thirteenth.
However, two years of negotiations were required before he
could be conveyed to Lhasa, as the Chinese warlord of Chinghai demanded 30,000 dollars before he would let the child
leave, and later upped it by another 90,000 dollars. In February, 1940, the four-and-a-half-year-old child was solemnly
installed as the Dalai Lama on the golden throne in the
Potala, and Sir Basil Gould, who headed the British delegation at this ceremony, remarked later on the child's com-
posure, poise, and gravity during the long hours of blessings
and prayers. When the Chinese invaded Tibet in October,
1950, the God-king was not quite sixteen, but it was decided
by his advisers to invest him with his full powers even though
he had not attained the recognized age for the conferment of
sovereignty. This was done on November 17, 1950, and on
December 18th the Dalai Lama left Lhasa for Yatung near
the Indian border, where he established a temporary government.

Second only in status and importance to the Dalai Lama is
the Panchen Lama who, as noted, was a creation of the fifth
Dalai Lama. The title actually conferred by the "Great Fifth"
on one of his revered teachers was Panchen Edreni (His Holiness the Great Teacher), but the Tibetans call him Panchen
Rimpoche (The Precious Grand Sage). The first Panchen
Lama was made the Grand Lama of the Tashi-lhunpo
monastery at Shigatse and proclaimed to be an incarnation
of Amitabha, "the Boundless Light" who is known in Tibet
as Opame. Since Amitabha was the spiritual guide of Avalokiteshwara, whose reincarnation is the Dalai Lama, the spiritual prestige of the Panchen Lama would appear to be higher

than that of the Dalai Lama. In theory, the Panchen Lama's functions are almost exclusively spiritual, his political authority being localized in the region around Shigatse, 130 miles west of Lhasa. In practice, however, foreign Powers—particularly China—have tended to use the Panchen Lama as a political foil against the Dalai Lama.

Just as the degree of Tibet's independence varied with the strength or weakness of the Chinese Government, so also the influence of the Panchen Lama has varied with the authority exercised by Peking. Whenever China was capable of exerting pressure on Tibet, the authority of the Dalai Lama has been weakened or compromised. Conversely, the Panchen Lama has tended to feel insecure when Tibet has been strong enough to resist Chinese threats or force. By and large the Panchen Lama has invariably looked to the Chinese for support against his temporal master in Tibet. And as invariably the Chinese have been quick to respond.

In the eighteenth century the dissensions which gave the Chinese an excuse to interfere in Tibet were caused largely by the differences and rivalries between the twin pillars of the Gelugpa sect—the Dalai Lama and the Panchen Lama. In 1780 the latter visited Peking for the Emperor Chien Lung's seventieth birthday and was given a reception comparable to that accorded to the fifth Dalai Lama a century earlier. The Tibetans interpreted this as a Chinese way of playing off the Panchen against the Dalai Lama, and for a while there was nervousness at Lhasa, but the Panchen Lama fortuitously died the same year of smallpox. When, again, in 1904 the thirteenth Dalai Lama fled to Mongolia from the British, the Chinese sought to "depose" him, and issued a proclamation to that effect which the Tibetans ignored. The Chinese also tried to install the Panchen Lama in the Dalai Lama's place, but this also the Tibetans ignored. On the Dalai Lama's return in 1909 the God-king found the Chinese

Resident Lien-Yu entrenched firmly in authority, and had difficulty in asserting his own. In 1910 he was again forced to flee—this time to India, as the Chinese demands grew more peremptory. The collapse of the Manchu Empire in 1911 enabled the Dalai Lama to return, expel the ambans and the Chinese forces, and by June, 1912, reestablish Tibetan authority completely. It is noticeable that when the God-king returned to Lhasa from his Indian exile he roundly rebuked the Panchen Lama for not fighting the Chinese garrison troops. Relations between the two grew so strained that in 1923 the Panchen Lama fled to China, where he died in exile in 1937.

In the fall of 1930 the then Kuomintang Government of China addressed eight questions to the Dalai Lama, seeking clarification of Sino-Tibetan relations and of the status of the Panchen Lama. The Dalai Lama's answers are illuminating. In reply to a question as to how good relations between Tibet and the Central Government might be restored, His Holiness answered: "If the Central Government would treat the patronage relationship between China and Tibet with sincerity and good faith, as it previously did, Tibet, on its part, having always shown sincerity in its dealings in the past, would from now on make an even greater effort to give full support to the Central Government." To another question regarding Tibet's autonomy the Dalai Lama's reply is even more emphatic: "The area over which autonomy is to be exercised should naturally be the same as before. It is expected that the Central Government will return to Tibet those districts which originally belonged to it, but which are under its control, so that a perpetual peace and harmony will surely be the result." And again regarding the Panchen Lama's status: "His duty has always been confined to the religious affairs of Tashi-lhunpo, for he has no political affairs to attend to. He should be available for membership of the Kuomintang.* It must be understood, however, that he has never had any say in the settlement of Tibetan affairs." The Dalai Lama also describes his relationship with the Panchen Lama as a "tutor-disciple relationship."

On December 17, 1933, the powerful thirteenth Dalai Lama died, and Tibet was again torn by factions and eyed covetously from abroad. If Tibet had got no nearer to the outside world, the outside world had got nearer to Tibet. Within the country there was rivalry between the strongly nationalist, forward-looking Young Tibet group and the vested interests of the monasteries which resented attempts to curtail their power. Abroad, China and Britain watched Tibet uneasily.

In the absence of the Dalai Lama a regent had to be elected, and the lamas succeeded in getting Reting Rimpoche, the abbot of a monastery, elected regent. But the Young Tibet group were influential with the army, and when the Chinese Nationalist Government attempted a *tour de force* by peremptorily demanding of Lhasa recognition of Peking's overlordship the Chinese were rebuffed. The demand was made through General Huang Mu-sung, who had been dispatched to Lhasa as Special Commissioner to Tibet, and the Tibetan reply was contained in a ten-point rejoinder. Some of the clauses of this document are revealing. The first point reads: "In dealing with external affairs, Tibet shall remain an integral part of the territory of China. But the Chinese Government must promise that Tibet will not be reorganized into a province." The Tibetans request that "the Chinese Government will not interfere with the Tibetan civil and military authorities. . . . One representative of the Chinese Government may be stationed in Tibet, but his retinue shall not exceed twenty-five. There shall be no other representative, either civil or military. This representative must be a

* The Panchen Lama was then in exile in China.

true believer in Buddhism." There is a reference to border-area disputes: "For permanent harmony and friendship, to avoid any possible disputes and to maintain peace on the borders, the northeastern boundary between Koko Nor and Tibet should be maintained as proposed during the negotiations of the year before last, with O-Lo, which has long been under Tibet, to be included on the Tibetan side. As for the boundary between Tibet and Szechwan, the territory and people, together with the administration of De-ge, Nyarong, and Tachienlu, should be turned over to the Tibetan Government at the earliest possible moment."

The Kuomintang Government, being in no position to force the issue, wisely held its hand. General Huang went back to Peking with no more than Lhasa's reluctant consent to the return of the Panchen Lama. When China attempted to secure the Panchen Lama's reentry into Tibet, the regent stalled. The problem was solved by the death of the Panchen Lama on December 1, 1937. But other problems arose. On February 22, 1940, the fourteenth Dalai Lama was installed at the Potala, and the opposition of the Young Tibet group to the regent Reting Rimpoche came to a head. In 1941 he retired in favor of Tagtra Rimpoche, head of a small monastery. Six years later the former regent, who had the backing of the monks of Sera monastery, attempted a revolt, which was quickly subdued and in which Reting Rimpoche lost his life in mysterious circumstances.

All these years, during the war and after, the Kuomintang Government, harassed by the Japanese and menaced by their own Communists, were too preoccupied to threaten Tibet. In August, 1945, Generalissimo Chiang Kai-shek conceded that "if and when the Tibetans attain the stage of complete self-reliance in political and economic conditions, the Chinese Government would like to take the same attitude as it did toward Outer Mongolia, by supporting their independence. . . . Tibet should be able to maintain and promote its own independent position in order that the historical tragedy of Korea might not be repeated." The tone of this declaration is more subdued than the ultimatum delivered to the Tibetans some five years earlier. History was repeating itself.

Though the Young Tibet group was able to keep China at bay, on one issue it was unable to assert itself. This concerned the choice of a new Panchen Lama, whose selection is governed roughly by the same procedure employed in the choice of a new Dalai Lama, and was similarly supervised by the Chinese representative at Lhasa. The ninth Panchen Lama, as noted, had died in exile in China in 1937. Search for his reincarnation was finally narrowed down to three boys, of whom one died before the selection was completed. Of the other two China backed one over whose choice Lhasa was not happy. Nonetheless he was installed in 1944 as the tenth Panchen Lama at the Kumbum monastery in the Chinese province of Chinghai. He is the present Panchen Lama, who, though selected by the Kuomintang Government, is subservient today to the Communists. There he follows tradition; for the Panchen Lama, like his predecessors, serves as China's Trojan horse in Tibet.

The tenth Panchen Lama, who is twenty-two, was born in Chinghai, a Chinese province carved out of Tibet a few generations earlier, and was declared a reincarnation of the ninth Panchen Lama in 1943. By a curious coincidence both he and the present Dalai Lama were born, or reincarnated, in the same province. While the Dalai Lama was taken to Lhasa at the age of four, the Panchen Lama remained in China until 1952 when he was brought by the Communists to Tibet for the first time and formally installed at the Tashi-lhunpo (Mount of Blessing) monastery at Shigatse. Slightly taller than the Dalai Lama, he is not as personable or pleasant, and lacks the graciousness and cultured charm of His Holiness. The Panchen Lama bears the honorific of His Serenity.

When the Communists seized power in China they were quick to exploit the Panchen Lama. Early in their advance across the Chinese mainland, the Chinese Communists announced that Tibet was an integral part of China and would be "liberated from the imperialists." In July, 1949, as the Communist troops were converging on Peking, the Tibetan Foreign Affairs Bureau politely asked the Chinese Nationalist Mission and all Chinese traders suspected of Communist sympathies to leave the country. Two months later the bureau requested Mao Tse-tung to respect Tibet's territorial integrity. Alive to the political value of the Panchen Lama, then a boy of twelve, the Chinese Communists began to cultivate him and his advisers, and when in October, 1950, the Communist armies marched into Tibet they persuaded the advisers to send a telegram from Chinghai in the Panchen Lama's name to Mao Tse-tung, by then Chairman of the Chinese People's Central Government, and to General Chu Teh, commander in chief of the People's Army, to express His Serenity's support for the "liberation" of Tibet. Shortly afterward the Panchen Lama was invited to Peking.

In January, 1950, General Chu Teh had declared China's decision to "liberate" Tibet from "imperialistic influences," and it was announced by the Chinese Government, two days after India had recognized the Communist regime, that one of the "basic tasks" of the People's Liberation Army during 1950 was the "liberation" of Tibet. Meanwhile the Tibetans reaffirmed their independence and hastily organized missions to rally support for Tibet's cause in India, Nepal, the United States, and Britain. Peking countered this move by a blunt warning that any country which received such an "illegal" mission would thereby demonstrate its hostility to

China. Eventually only a single seven-man mission, appointed by the Dalai Lama's Government, left in April, 1950, for India en route to Hong Kong, where it hoped to meet representatives of the Peking Government. The British authorities, however, refused to grant visas to the Tibetans on the ground that such negotiations might exacerbate the already "delicate situation" in Hong Kong, and the mission consequently found itself marooned in Kalimpong.

The first Chinese Communist ambassador arrived at New Delhi in September, and on Lhasa's instructions the Tibetan mission opened negotiations with him, but the talks ended inconclusively on October 1st. According to one report the Tibetans were offered a choice between immediate surrender or invasion and given to understand that nothing less than incorporation of Tibet within the "new China" would be acceptable. Peking demanded that the delegation should come to the Chinese capital. As is their habit when placed in difficult situations, the Tibetans played for time, and Peking characteristically construed the delay as due to hostile foreign intrigue and interference.

India had all along counseled that the Sino-Tibetan dispute should be settled peacefully. On October 25, 1950, the Tibetan delegation left Delhi, and almost simultaneously came the news that the "People's Liberation Army units have been ordered to advance into Tibet." India protested at this use of *force majeure* but was curtly told by the Chinese to mind her own business.

Actually the Chinese armies had marched into Tibet on October 7th, crossing the headwaters of the Yangtze, Mekong, and Salween rivers at several points simultaneously on that day, and had attacked isolated garrisons on the outer fringe of the Tibetan fortress town of Chamdo. This town is in the eastern region of Kham and was once part of Sikang Province, which no longer exists. At Chang-tu, about ninety miles from the Sino-Tibetan frontier, the Tibetans made a valiant but vain attempt to defend their country. According to the Chinese some four thousand men and officers were taken prisoner or killed by the People's Army. Among those captured was the governor of the Chamdo area, Ngabon Ngawang Jigme, who was also a member of the Kashag. He was subjected by the Communists to some months of "brain-washing," and proved a docile pupil, for, as noted, he was one of two members of the Kashag who did not accompany the Dalai Lama when His Holiness fled to India in March, 1959.

Chamdo fell on October 13th, and there was little resistance by the Tibetans after that. The main military defense of Tibet had been breached, and thereafter the Chinese advanced in a leisurely way, one army moving from Central China through the former Sikang Province, the other from northwestern China through Chinghai Province—both converging on Lhasa and both building highways as they advanced. Late in April, 1951, a delegation of six Tibetans, led by the pro-Chinese Ngabon Ngawang Jigme, arrived in Peking from Lhasa, and on May 23, 1951, the Communist-imposed seventeen-point agreement was signed. We shall examine this later. During the negotiations and after, the tenth Panchen Lama, along with some forty of his followers, was present at Peking. It was said after Napoleon's fall that the Allies had brought the Bourbons back to France in their baggage. The Panchen Lama was to go to Tibet with the Chinese as their creature.

Meanwhile, on August 8, 1951, the first official representative of the Peking regime, General Chang Ching-wu, arrived at Lhasa, a month ahead of the vanguard of the Chinese Army. Nine days later the Dalai Lama returned from Yatung to the Potala, but not until October 24th did he officially intimate to Mao Tse-tung the Tibetan Government's acceptance of the May 23rd agreement. On October 26th the divisions of the People's Army which had entered Tibet from the east marched into Lhasa under Lieutenant General Chang Kuo-hua, and they were reinforced on December 1st by the divisions which had entered Tibet from the northwest. On February 10, 1952, the Tibet Military District of the Communist Chinese Army was formally established at Lhasa under the command of General Chang. China's military stranglehold on Tibet was complete.

Before examining in detail the developments from Communist China's invasion of Tibet in 1950 to the flight of the Dalai Lama in 1959, let us look at the governmental structure of Tibet as it was prior to the Communist infiltration.

Under the Dalai Lama, Tibet was divided for administrative purposes into five main zones which in turn were subdivided into several provinces and districts. The five main zones were U-Tsang (Lhasa and Shigatse), Gartok (western Tibet), Kham (eastern Tibet), Loka (southern Tibet), and Chang (northern Tibet). In each of these zones was a representative of the government known as *chi-kyap*. Below the chi-kyaps were the *dzongpons* (captains of the fortresses) who act as local magistrates and tax collectors. These officials, both at the top and lower levels, could be either lay or clerical, monks figuring in the civil and military administration.

The ultimate control of all civil and ecclesiastical matters lay in the hands of the Dalai Lama, whose authority was supreme. During his minority or absence a regent who was appointed by the Tsongdu (National Assembly) could act for the Dalai Lama; but no one else, including the Panchen Lama, may exercise his temporal or religious authority. The regent chosen was traditionally an Incarnate Lama from one of seven specified monasteries.

Like the Dalai Lama, who exercised both secular and ecclesiastical authority, so also the administration retained a dual character, with a secular and an ecclesiastical official functioning jointly at each post. During the periods when the Dalai Lama ruled (but not when there was a Regent), there were usually two prime ministers, one an ecclesiastical prime minister and the other a prime minister of state for civil affairs. They were known as *silons,* and served as intermediaries between the Kashag and the Dalai Lama. One of the first moves of the Chinese Communists was to dismiss the Dalai Lama's two prime ministers, Lukhang, a nobleman, and Lobsang Tashi, a lama.

The Kashag (Tibetan Cabinet) originally consisted of four members, one a monk and three nobles who are known as *shapes* or *kalons.* Later the number was enlarged to six, four of them lay and two monks. Each member held one or more portfolios in the government, but matters of foreign policy were under the direct charge of the Dalai Lama, though in 1942 a Bureau of Foreign Affairs under the state prime minister was created. The Chinese Communists compelled the Kashag to dissolve the bureau. On the secular side of the government was an Accounting Office composed of four *tsepons* (chief accountants or financial secretaries), and the secular side of the government also supervised the provincial governors (*depons*) with their subordinate prefects known as dzongpons, a pair consisting of a monk and a layman, who were in charge of the districts (dzongs) into which the country was divided.

The ecclesiastical counterpart of the Kashag was the Yiktsang (Nest of Letters), and this body was composed entirely of monks, normally four in number. The Yiktsang holds the Dalai Lama's seal, which is affixed to all documents of importance, and also appointed the monks who shared power with the lay nobles at the higher rungs of the administrative ladder. It administered all the monasteries except the Three Great ones (Drepung, Sera, and Ganden). The Lord Chamberlain (Chi-kyap Khempo) who was in charge of the Potala was the counterpart of the silons and acted as intermediary between the Yiktsang and the Dalai Lama. The present Dalai Lama's third elder brother, Lobsang Samten, who had been with His Holiness to Yatung, held the office of Lord Chamberlain. The treasuries within the Potala were in charge of the ecclesiastical section of the government.

Assisting the Kashag was the Tsongdu, or National Assembly, which was summoned by the Kashag only to discuss matters of great national importance. Its functions were advisory, its decisions being transmitted through the Kashag, which could add its own recommendations, to the Dalai Lama. In this assembly the opinions of the abbots and treasurers of the Three Great Monasteries carried the largest weight. The Tsongdu had some 350 members made up of an equal proportion of priests and laymen. A Small Assembly (Tsongdu Dupa) composed of about forty laymen and twenty monks was occasionally invited to discuss matters of lesser importance.

Despite the centralized character of the administration, the degree of local autonomy in Tibet's outlying areas depended largely on the personality and prestige of the Dalai Lama. Of the modern Dalai Lamas the greatest so far has been the thirteenth, ranking only second to the Great Fifth. The peculiar misfortune of Tibet has been that at a crucial period of her history, when the Hans who were hammering down the door finally forced it open, both the Dalai Lama and the Panchen Lama were minors, for in 1950 the Dalai Lama was around fifteen while the Panchen Lama was a little over twelve. Both were susceptible to environment and influence.

It cannot be denied that the numerical preponderance of

the lamas and their pervasive influence in the secular and ecclesiastical spheres, combined with the fact that the monasteries relied mainly on the lay population for financial support, even though the state had endowed them generously with landed property, rendered this class a heavy burden on the people. They enjoyed many privileges which attracted not a few masculine drones to the profession of priesthood. The Chinese Government, even before the Communists came to power, realized the political value of Tibet's vast army of lamas and monks, and capitalized on it by heavily subsidizing various monasteries, including the three great seats which in moments of stress could be relied upon to support them. This has paid dividends no less in the days of the Manchus than of Mao Tse-tung.

Since the Communist offensive has been concentrated largely on the lamas, it is necessary to peer more closely at the social and religious structure of Lamaism, which is Tibet's religion. That the monks form a superior caste is evident in and acknowledged by the fact that wherever they share authority with a layman—and this is widespread in Tibetan administration—the voice of the monk prevails. On the other hand, the procedure which governs the selection of the Dalai Lama combines both conservative and liberal practices respecting the aristocratic and democratic. It also ensures a measure of social stability. In so far as the Dalai Lama may emerge from economically the lowest in the land—the Great Fifth was the son of a poor peasant from Chung-gye—the method of his selection makes for national unity. There is no class consciousness where the Living Buddha is concerned. His office is no one's privilege. And the manner of his choice combines respect for popular democracy with regard for metaphysical monarchy, perhaps deliberately, since if he came from a rich family its automatic ennoblement might tend to make an already influential family excessively powerful.

Tibetan life has been medieval and feudal. But, oddly enough, the Tibetans seem to be among the really happy people of the world, which is not an excuse for perpetuating prevailing social and economic conditions but a sound reason for inducing change within the pattern of Tibetan thinking, though not by the imposition of a cast-iron Chinese mold.

To the average Tibetan his religion is what really matters. "The one thing," said a refugee, "which the Chinese want to break is our worship of our Gods. That is why we left." And another, pulling out from beneath his shirt a string of bags with sacred relics which encircled his neck, remarked, "If my heart is pure, fifty bullets can't kill me." The strength and influence wielded by the monasteries, which are the strongholds of Lamaism, are undoubtedly enormous. There are over three thousand of these in Tibet. But Lamaism as practiced is a living faith, not merely the privilege and perquisite of an ambitious and avaricious monastic brotherhood, but a truly popular religion which saturates the life and mind of the Tibetan people.

Actually, the form of Buddhism practiced in Tibet is not vastly different from Indian Buddhism, being of the same type as the Mahayana or theistic form of Buddhism. First in order of importance in the Lamaist pantheon is the Buddha, then Amitabha, whose reincarnation is the Panchen Lama; and next Avalokiteshwara, whose spirit lives in the Dalai Lama. Highest in the Lamaist pantheon is the Adi Buddha, or First Buddha—the One, the External, the Uncreated. In Tibet he is known by different names representative of different attributes. Thus the Gelugpa sect call him Dorje-chang (He Who Holds the Lightning), while the Ngingmapa or Kadamba sect call him Samantabhadra (Universal Kindness). The Kargyupa lamas, who practice an oral tradition, know him as Dorje-sempa (Whose Essence Is

Light). The Adi Buddha has five manifestations, the Five Dhyani Buddhas (Buddhas of meditation), each presiding over one of the five *kalpas* (epochs) * of the world, and each emanating one of the five elements, one of the five senses, one of the five colors, and one of the five vowels. These Dhyani Buddhas are depicted as ascetics seated in the Adamantine posture, the posture of most meditation. They represent the thought and order behind our multiple universe. Each Dhyani Buddha has his Dhyani Bodhisattva whom he generates, and each Dhyani Bodhisattva creates a universe over which he presides, and has two aspects— *samsara* (militant) and *karuna* (benevolent compassion). Once in every epoch each Dhyani Buddha generates a Manushi Buddha, a terrestrial Buddha like Gautama himself, who was born Prince Siddhartha and became the Lord Buddha. Succession by reincarnation governs the line of the two Grand Lamas, who are linked in a metaphysical interdependence representing two aspects of the Buddha—the Panchen Lama being an incarnation of the Dhyani Buddha Amitabha while the Dalai Lama is the incarnation of the Dhyani Bodhisattva Avalokiteshwara. The Bodhisattvas, being potential Buddhas, are in contact with the vortex of life, while a Dhyani Buddha lives only on the plane of pure thought. This is the reason why the Panchen Lama is supposed to wield no secular power, confining himself only to the spiritual, though it does not always happen in practice. The Dalai Lama exercises both spiritual and secular authority.

Everywhere in Tibet one sees inscribed or hears chanted the sacred words *Om Mane Padme Hum,* which translated literally mean "Hail to the Jewel in the Lotus."

Yet as an Incarnate Lama explained to an Indian visitor,

* Lamaists reckon the present to be the fourth epoch. Each epoch runs into thousands of years.

"The Jewel is none else but the Buddha, and the Lotus is the heart. So its real rendering is 'Hail to the Buddha in our hearts!'"

God, according to the Tibetans, resides in every one of their hearts.

the
dragon
leaps
forward

CHAPTER THREE

"Recognizing that each nationality has the right to self-determination does not mean that each nationality must be independent and isolated," declared Radio Peking in the first of two lectures on "Basic Marxism-Leninism" delivered on May 9, 1956. "Whether it is appropriate for a nationality to be independent . . . is for the Communist party to decide. Lenin expressed the essence of the right of nations to self-determination in a simple formula: 'To separate in order to unite.' "

On May 10th, in the course of the second lecture, the speaker observed: "The various national minorities are politically, economically, and culturally backward as compared to the Han nationality. They live in extensive areas of rich natural resources, highly significant to the socialist construction of the motherland. . . . In accordance with the

64

situation the Chinese Communist party formulated its policy toward nationalities. This is a policy to consolidate . . . and build up the great motherland."

Five years earlier the Chinese Communists had applied this policy to Tibet, emphasizing in the preamble to the Sino-Tibetan agreement of May 23, 1951, that "in order that the Tibetan nationality and people might be freed and return to the big family of the People's Republic of China to enjoy the same rights of national equality as all the other nationalities in the country," the seventeen-point agreement was being signed. In effect this declaration implied two things—first, that Tibet had not before this, for some time at least, been a member of the big family of the great motherland and, second, that the agreement was between two equal and independent countries. For instance, the preamble to the agreement states, *inter alia,* that "the Central People's Government appointed representatives with full powers to conduct talks on a friendly basis with the delegates with full powers of the local government of Tibet. As a result of these talks both parties agreed to conclude this agreement and carry it into effect." The reference to "full powers" implies an independent and equal status for both sides which is reinforced by the fact that the essential purpose of the agreement was not the grant of power by the Chinese Government to the Government of Tibet but the transfer of certain rights by Tibet to the Chinese authorities. In order to be able to transfer rights a state must possess them more specifically under Article 14 of the agreement. Tibet undertook to surrender to China her right to conduct her foreign affairs, a right which automatically carries with it an international status and recognition.

To turn to the agreement itself. Clause 1, accordingly, says: "The Tibetan people shall unite and drive out imperialist aggressive forces from Tibet; the Tibetan people shall return to the big family of the Motherland—the People's Republic of China." Since the agreement was a result of aggression by the imperialist Chinese, the irony of the clause was perhaps noted but not relished by the Tibetans. In return for this gesture the Chinese conceded that "the Tibetan people have the right of exercising national regional autonomy under the unified leadership of the Central People's Government." The content and character of this national regional autonomy was indicated negatively by Chinese promises not to interfere in certain spheres.

Thus Clause 4 specifically stated that "the central authorities will not alter the existing political system in Tibet. The central authorities also will not alter the established status, functions, and powers of the Dalai Lama. Officials of various ranks shall hold office as usual."

Clause 5 ensures that the established status, functions, and powers of the Panchen Lama shall be maintained; while the following clause, interpreting what is meant by the established status, functions, and powers of these two Grand Lamas, defines them as those enjoyed by the thirteenth Dalai Lama and the ninth Panchen Lama when they were in friendly and amicable relations with each other. Clause 7 promises that "the religious beliefs, customs, and habits of the Tibetan people shall be respected, and the lama monasteries shall be protected. The central authorities will not affect a change in the income of the monasteries."

There is yet another promise which the Chinese Communists must have given with their tongues well in their cheeks. Under Clause 11 they pledge that "in matters related to various reforms in Tibet, there will be no compulsion on the part of the central authorities. The local Government of Tibet shall carry out reforms of its own accord, and when the people raise demands for reform they shall be settled by means of consultation with the leading personnel of Tibet."

These promises were no sooner given than they were broken. Yet with characteristic cynicism the Chinese Communists continued to give bland assurances of their intention to respect Tibetan autonomy. In a reference to projected land reforms, Mao Tse-tung while receiving a Tibetan delegation in 1952 assured them that "it is as yet premature to speak of distributing the land in Tibet. The Tibetan people themselves must decide whether it is to be distributed in the future. Moreover the land, when it is distributed, will be distributed by the Tibetan people themselves." Such assurances were probably provoked by the growing resistance in Tibet to the Communist policy of infiltration, indoctrination, and domination, a conclusion supported by similar statements made by lesser Chinese dignitaries with the sole intention of allaying Tibetan fears and suspicions while pressing Communist policies forward. This was virtually admitted by General Chang Kuo-hua, commander of the Tibet military district, in a speech at Lhasa some three weeks after the Dalai Lama's flight when he confessed that Tibetan resistance to Communist "reforms" had begun as early as 1951. Nonetheless in the late fall of 1954, when the Indian prime minister was in Peking, Mao Tse-tung utilized the opportunity to stage a pantomime of his own. In the presence of Mr. Nehru he assured the Dalai Lama, who was there with the Panchen Lama, that Tibet would enjoy autonomy which "no other Chinese province enjoyed in the People's Republic of China." Earlier, on September 20th, when the Chinese ruler received the two Grand Lamas he had indicated that among impending changes the Chinese intended to colonize Tibet at a ratio of around five to one. This was disclosed two years later in a speech at Lhasa on April 26,

1956, by General Chang Kuo-hua, who paraphrased Mao's statement: "Tibet is a huge area but is too thinly populated. Efforts must be made to raise the population from the present level of two million to more than ten million. Besides, the economy and culture need development. Under the heading of culture, schools, newspapers, films, and so on, are included, and also religion. . . ."

The last clause of the Sino-Tibetan agreement stipulated that it "shall come into force immediately after signatures and seals are affixed to it," which implied that it would not be operative unless and until the Dalai Lama's seal was affixed to the document. Accordingly the Tibetan delegates, accompanied by one of the Chinese signatories, Chang Ching-wu, proceeded to Yatung, where the Dalai Lama had moved his government from Lhasa. They arrived there on July 14, 1951, and showed the document to His Holiness, who in August decided to return to his capital, reaching it on August 17th. He did not, however, formally accept it until October 24th. As the God-king explained to the world press in his statement issued from Mussoorie on June 20, 1959: "While I and my Government did not voluntarily accept the agreement, we were obliged to acquiesce in it and decided to abide by the terms and conditions in order to save my people and country from danger of total destruction. It was, however, clear from the very beginning that the Chinese had no intention of carrying out the agreement." His Holiness at the same time alleged that the Tibetan seal affixed to the agreement "was not the seal of my representatives but a seal copied and fabricated by the Chinese authorities in Peking and kept in their possession ever since."

If this is correct, the Dalai Lama's approval of the agreement was not only obtained under duress but enforced by chicanery. That it was obtained under duress is clear from the three-month interval which occurred between the submission of the document to His Holiness and the God-king's reluctant consent. The Dalai Lama did not accept the agreement until after the vanguard units of the People's Liberation Army arrived in Lhasa on September 9, 1951, and the main body of the army was on the outskirts of the capital. Significantly, too, the Tibetans attached no validity to the agreement until the Dalai Lama had formally assented. Why in the circumstances the Chinese should have fabricated the God-king's seal which should have been attached to the agreement is less easily explained. It is possible that the Yiktsang, which holds the Dalai Lama's seal in custody, was reluctant to transport it to Peking and that the Chinese, interpreting this as the traditional Tibetan method of playing for time, forestalled it by devices of their own.

Having established the Tibet Military Area Headquarters in February, 1952, and opened the Lhasa branch of the People's Bank of China in the same month, the Communists around April began to assert their authority more overtly. The Dalai Lama was first compelled to dismiss his two prime ministers under the threat, as he revealed at Mussoorie, "of their execution without trial because they had in all honesty and sincerity resisted unjustified usurpation of power by the representatives of the Chinese Government in Tibet." The Kashag, as noted, was also ordered to dissolve its Foreign Affairs Bureau, and was replaced by a Lhasa Foreign Affairs Office of the Peking regime, "to dispose of all foreign affairs of the Tibet area." This, however, was in accord with the agreement.

Having accomplished this, the Chinese Communists then set out systematically to erode the powers of the Dalai Lama and enlarge those of the Panchen Lama. On April 28, 1952, the Panchen Lama, never previously in Tibet, was brought to Lhasa under the auspices of the People's Liberation Army and formally installed later in the Tashi-lhunpo monastery at Shigatse. The Dalai Lama's prestige and power were still considerable, however, and the Chinese, behind a façade of Tibetan representation, could only bypass these by subtly altering the governmental structure to enlarge the Panchen Lama's domain and authority and simultaneously to curtail those of the Dalai Lama.

They did this in three ways over a period extending from 1951 to 1956. In 1951 the Chinese Communists organized the People's Liberation Committee of the Chamdo Area, where their armies had first penetrated when they had invaded Tibet the year before. This area in the western half of what was then Sikang Province was formerly governed from Lhasa by the Tibetan Government.* It now came under the control of the Liberation Committee, which set up its own organs of administration at the local and regional levels, abolished the "feudal service systems" of the former government, and established state trading companies and controlled schools. Five years later, when the Communists set up the Preparatory Committee of the Tibetan Autonomous Area, which effectively neutralized the Dalai Lama's authority, the People's Liberation Committee was one of its three component units. One of the other two was the local Tibetan Government headed by the Dalai Lama, and the third was to be the Panchen Kanpo Lija, under the Panchen Lama's control.

In March, 1954, the Communists established at Shigatse, seat of the Panchen Lama, the so-called Panchen Kanpo Lija, or Council, staffed by followers of the Panchen Lama whose primary loyalty was to His Serenity and not to His Holiness. The exact extent of the territory administered by the Panchen Kanpo Lija was never defined, but it covered the populous sections of the province of Tsang, which forms a

---

* Sikang Province was abolished on July 18, 1955, and incorporated partly into Tibet and partly into Szechwan Province.

large portion of central Tibet. Of about 200,000 people in Tsang, the Panchen Lama's followers number over 100,000.

Thus by 1954 Tibet was divided into three administrative areas, over only one of which the Dalai Lama, with his seat at Lhasa, exercised effective authority. Even this restricted power, as noted, was neutralized by the establishment in Lhasa on April 22, 1956, of the Preparatory Committee for the Tibet Autonomous Region, whose creation had been first authorized by the Chinese State Council in March, 1955. The Chinese division of Tibet into three administrative areas added a new element to the existing Han-Tibetan rivalries —intra-Tibetan disunity, which was crystallized, fostered, and accentuated by the establishment of the Preparatory Committee.

Of the fifty-one members of the Preparatory Committee, fifteen represented the local Tibetan Government, which was under the Dalai Lama's control, while ten were from the Panchen Kanpo Lija and ten from the People's Liberation Committee of the Chamdo area. In addition there were five members from the cadres of the Central People's Government now working in the Tibet area, and eleven others, including representatives from the major monasteries, religious sects, and public bodies. The Dalai Lama was appointed director, with the Panchen Lama and General Chang Kuo-hua as first and second vice directors. Simultaneously, the Chinese made it clear that the Preparatory Committee would function under the direction of the State Council at Peking. On administrative matters (a compendious and comprehensive term) the three organizations—the local Tibetan Government, the Panchen Kanpo Lija, and the People's Liberation Committee of the Chamdo Area—were also directly responsible to the Chinese State Council. It was, moreover, stipulated that all the enterprises under the State Council which operated in Tibet would be controlled by the various responsible departments of the State Council, and that the agency for carrying out the State Council's directives would be the PLA Tibetan Military District Command. Thereby Tibet's administrative matters were in practice controlled by the Chinese Army authorities, though theoretically the power resided in a body with a façade of Tibetan representation. Many of the committee's subordinate offices were headed by Chinese Communists. Of forty-nine "leadership personnel" seventeen were Chinese and thirty-two Tibetans, while according to the list released by the New China News Agency a Chinese was among the "leadership personnel" of every one of the fifteen committees except that of Culture-Education. This office, however, was in the safe hands of the Political Committee of the Tibet Military Command. As the Dalai Lama observed in his statement of June 20th at Mussoorie, "They [the Chinese Communists] did not lose any opportunity to undermine my authority and sow dissension among my people."

Behind the façade of Tibetan autonomy the Chinese worked methodically to undermine the Dalai Lama's influence in every sphere. Before the end of 1952 branches of the People's Bank of China were opened in the principal cities and towns of Tibet. On May 1, 1952, the Chinese created the Tibet Regional Working Committee of the Communist Youth League to aid their efforts to indoctrinate the country's youth who they felt could be most easily "educated" into accepting Chinese rule and the Marxist philosophy. Simultaneously they planned to utilize this new youthful cadre to eliminate education in the Buddhist religion and deprecate other traditional Tibetan social values. By January, 1953, a New China News Agency dispatch was able to claim that fourteen primary schools with thirteen hundred pupils had been opened and over four hundred Tibetans trained. Hundreds of Tibetan youths were taken to China for "training," and returned to their country duly indoctrinated. In April, 1957, the Chinese Communists claimed that during the past six years some seventy primary schools with accommodation for six thousand students had been established in various localities in Tibet.

Propaganda proceeded with indoctrination. By 1953 the Political Department of the Tibet Military District had begun publication of a monthly paper called *Tibetan News,* and this was reinforced three years later in April, 1956, by a daily, the Tibet *Jih Pao,* published in Tibetan and Chinese, which served as the organ of the Preparatory Committee. Many thousands of handouts of propaganda material in the Tibetan language were distributed by PLA units in various parts of the country.

Yet even here, in propaganda and indoctrination, on which the Communists concentrated from the beginning, the Tibetans offered resistance. Until the Communists came, education in Tibet was practically non-existent except in a religious form, and was confined to the monks, nobles, merchants, and other affluent classes. Many Tibetan monks are educated and well versed in the complexities of Lamaism and Tibetan politics. For the most part the nobles and others of their ilk are educated partly in Tibet by monks and partly abroad, in English-teaching schools in India. In 1913 Sir Charles Bell, British Representative at Lhasa, persuaded the Tibetan Government to send four Tibetan boys for education to England. One of the four was Dorje Tsegyal Lungshar, who for a brief period after the thirteenth Dalai Lama's death was the dominating political force in Tibet.

For the serfs and artisans there were no educational facilities, and the Communists have concentrated on them as good and pliable material for their purposes. At the new Lhasa Primary School the children of the aristocracy now sit alongside the children of the serfs, and about two-thirds of the pupils come from the homes of commoners. The pattern is repeated in the one hundred and more primary schools which the Communists have established in the country. These institutions are coeducational. No religious instruction is now given, but there is a course on the Han language. In more advanced educational institutions, such as the colleges of social education at Lhasa and Shigatse, political studies have a high place in the curriculum and consist largely in the study of Sino-Tibetan agreements (particularly the agreement of 1951), the Chinese Constitution, and the policy of the Chinese Communist Government on religion and national minorities. The Communists have also set up technical colleges, devoted largely to agriculture and livestock farming—the two main branches of Tibetan economy —and institutions for training in administration, medicine, banking, and industry.

In themselves these are welcome reforms, and would have been accepted as such by the vast mass of Tibetans had their objective not been the undermining and eventual uprooting of the Tibetan religion, culture, and way of life and the indoctrination of the country's youth with Communist ideas. In his June 20th statement at Mussoorie the Dalai Lama declared that the Tibetan Government was not opposed to reforms. Indeed, it realized the need for them. "I wish to emphasize," said His Holiness, "that I and my government have never been opposed to reforms which are necessary in the social, economic, and political systems prevailing in Tibet. We have no desire to disguise the fact that ours is an ancient society and that we must introduce immediate changes in the interests of the people of Tibet." The Dalai Lama went on to say that during the previous nine years he and his government had proposed several reforms but that the Chinese had strenuously resisted them and prevented their realization.

The only reforms the Communists were prepared to introduce were those molded to suit Marxist ends. What the Chinese aimed at in Tibet was the production of reliable pro-Chinese Communists, and this involved a complete break with Tibetan traditions. The zeal with which the Chinese carried out this indoctrination is revealed in a report submitted late in 1957 by Fan Ming, Secretary of the Chinese Communist party's Tibet Work Committee. "Now," he reports, "there are more than 5,000 local revolutionary cadres of Tibetan nationality, more than 1,000 Communist party members of Tibetan nationality, and more than 2,000 Youth Communist League members. At the same time, there are more than 6,000 members of the Patriotic Youth Cultural Association, and more than 1,000 members of the Patriotic Women's Association." Members of the last two associations, apart from their collective activities, were required to set up home study groups in each village. The Tibet *Jih Pao* of December 11, 1957, carried a report of the activities of one such association at Yatung: "They not only study policy on 'no reform in six years,' * but also study articles on major foreign and home events carried in the Tibetan edition of the Tibet *Jih Pao*. The Yatung branch of the C.C.P. Work Committee gave them reading materials."

The same Fan Ming about this time was driven to confess that the problem of Chinese disregard for Tibetan customs and sensitivities was becoming worse, and that Tibetan resentment was increasing. "Great-Han chauvinism in Tibet," he complained, "is manifested in the feeling of superiority of the Han race, repugnance at the backwardness of Tibet, discrimination against Tibet, distortion of Tibet, failure to respect the freedom of religious belief and traditional customs of the Tibetan people. . . . As a result, some cases

* This refers to the Chinese decision, announced in 1957, not to proceed with "democratic reforms" in Tibet until after 1962.

have occurred where the nationalities policy was impaired, law and discipline were violated, and the freedom of religious belief and the customs of the Tibetans were not respected." The Communist phrase for describing these lapses was to label them "the phenomenon of commandism."

Not long after the Dalai Lama's flight a communiqué issued by Peking on March 28, 1959, admitted that Tibetan officials had begun to organize resistance to Communism soon after the Chinese armies had entered Tibet. It declared that ever since 1951 highly placed Tibetans, including four of the six members of the Kashag, had "been plotting to tear up the [seventeen-point] agreement and preparing for armed rebellion." This was later reiterated by the Chinese Communist military commander in Tibet, General Chang Kuo-hua, who revealed in a speech on April 8, 1959, to the Preparatory Committee that the Tibetan Government's opposition to Communist policies began soon after the Sino-Tibetan agreement of 1951 was signed. According to Chang, "a group of reactionaries" headed by Sitzub Lokangwa, Tsewong Routen, and Lozong Drashi of the former local Tibetan Government had in 1952 organized a people's conference with the intention of starting a counterrevolutionary plot. This group had submitted a memorandum to the Chinese through the Dalai Lama demanding that His Holiness should be given full control over Tibet, that the over-all strength of the Chinese occupation troops should be reduced, that conditions in the Tibetan monasteries should be improved, and that the food situation should be seriously considered because food prices were rising dizzily. Not only had the local Tibetan Government failed to deal with the "reactionaries," but it had, alleged Chang, actively connived with and supported them. The general was referring to the Tibetan patriotic organization called Mimang, which means in Tibetan the "masses" or the "majority."

Thus opposition to the Chinese Communists was by no means confined, as they asserted later, to the feudal minority, but was widespread among the people. On this point Mr. Nehru shared the Tibetan view, and said so in his speech to the Lok Sabha on April 27, 1959: "To say that a number of 'upper strata reactionaries' in Tibet were solely responsible for this appears to be an extraordinary simplification of a complicated situation. Even according to the accounts received through Chinese sources, the revolt in Tibet was of considerable magnitude and the basis of it must have been a strong feeling of nationalism which affects not only the upper-class people, but others also. No doubt, vested interests joined it and sought to profit by it. The attempt to explain a situation by the use of rather worn-out words, phrases, and slogans is seldom helpful."

Naturally the Chinese Communists did not relish the Indian prime minister's frank statement. But Nehru's analysis had in fact been earlier borne out by the declarations of the Chinese leaders themselves, including Mao Tse-tung and Chou En-lai, the former having ordered a tactical retreat in Tibet in his famous speech on "contradictions" on February 27, 1957. "Because conditions in Tibet are not ripe, democratic reforms have not yet been carried out there," explained Chairman Mao. "It has now been decided not to proceed with democratic reform in Tibet during the period of the second Five-Year Plan,* and we can only decide whether it will be done in the third Five-Year Plan in the light of the situation obtaining at that time." On April 22, 1957—the first anniversary of the formation of the Preparatory Committee—a government decree formally announced that social reforms in Tibet would be postponed until after 1962. If opposition to them had been confined only to the upper strata, Peking would not have bowed even temporarily before

* The second Five-Year Plan was initiated in 1957.

the storm. In fact the Tibet *Jih Pao* of August 23, 1957, admitted that the opposition was widespread. "Although a minority of the people is eager for the reforms, the majority still lacks an enthusiastic demand," it confessed.

One of the Communists' earliest activities was to open up Tibet—to China. In that sense the former state of geographical isolation was replaced by one of political insulation. The improvement of communications with China by air, rail, and land enjoys a high priority in the Communist development programs, for politically and economically it brings Tibet closer within the Han fold.

As the Chinese troops advanced into Tibet in the late fall of 1950, they were directed by Peking to undertake, with the help of the "work personnel" also entering Tibet, the construction of two major arteries to link Tibet with China. These were the Sikang-Tibet and the Chinghai-Tibet highways, the former linking Lhasa with Central China, the latter connecting the Tibetan capital with northwestern China. Both represent considerable engineering feats, the 1,413-mile Sikang-Tibet highway being reckoned the world's highest road, perched at an average height of 13,000 feet across fourteen high mountain ranges and twelve rivers, including the Mekong and the Salween. The Chinghai-Tibet highway also traverses difficult terrain over the desolate swampland and desert of northern Tibet, running from Sining east of Lake Koko Nor to Zamsar about fifty miles northwest of Lhasa. The two highways meet at Zamsar from where the Sikang-Tibet road has been extended southwest to Shigatse and through Gyantse to Phari, the nearest town from the mouth of Nathu La, the old caravan pass leading to Gangtok, capital of Sikkim, which lies some thirty miles on the other side of the border. Northward the Tibet-Sikang highway reaches out from Sining by an older highway to Lanchow in the Chinese province of Kansu.

Both these highways were completed by December, 1954, and according to Radio Peking "the journey from Peking or Shanghai to Lhasa has been cut to less than twenty days as compared with three months needed by the old caravan routes." On the Sikang-Tibet highway the first convoy of trucks, again according to Radio Peking, took eight days to go from Chengtu, where the road begins, to the southern bank of a tributary of the river Kyi Chu which runs through Lhasa. This journey had formerly taken "more than thirty-eight days." The extension of the Sikang highway from Lhasa to Shigatse, seat of the Panchen Lama, and beyond almost to the Bhutan-Sikkimese border is indicative of the Communists' political motives and their calculated efforts to increase the authority of the Panchen Lama at the cost of the Dalai Lama. The extension of the road to Shigatse meant that one could drive from there to Lhasa within a day, a journey which had formerly taken a week by horse. The political influence of the Panchen Lama could thereby make a proportionately closer impact. On the economic side Shigatse was put on the main route from India to Lhasa and Peking, and its economic importance was consequently increased.

It is evident that the Dalai Lama and his advisers were not unaware of these implications, for despite continuous, even rigorous, Communist control and supervision His Holiness was able by subtle suggestion in his public statements to indicate that he did not wholly approve of Chinese policies. He had noted that while the Communists sought to denigrate his political authority vis-à-vis the Panchen Lama, they had also attempted unsuccessfully to deprecate his spiritual influence. In May, 1954, both the Grand Lamas were summoned to Peking for the First National People's Congress as deputies from Tibet, and in August they left the country by different routes for the Chinese capital. In their absence the Communists began a campaign against the Dalai Lama, even rewriting Tibetan Buddhist history to suggest that the Panchen Lama was the ruler of Outer Tibet, which includes the Lhasa region, while the Dalai Lama's authority was alleged to be restricted to the disputed districts of Inner Tibet, which comprise areas in Chinghai, Szechwan, and Kansu provinces. These efforts did not impress the Tibetans, but it is noteworthy that the Chinese Communist attempts to whittle down the Dalai Lama's prestige extended to Chinese-populated areas abroad. About this time, in 1954, the Hong Kong Communist daily *Ta Kung Pao* blatantly declared that after the death of Tsong-kapa, founder of the Gelugpa sect of Yellow Hats, "two of his disciples ruled over Inner and Outer Tibet respectively in accordance with his will. The elder disciple, the Dalai Lama, became ruler of Inner Tibet and the younger disciple, the Panchen Lama, ruler of Outer Tibet." These palpable efforts to diminish the Dalai Lama's prestige were not unnoticed by him.

The two major highways linking Tibet with China, as well as the network of new roads inside Tibet, were described by the Chinese as having been constructed by voluntary labor. In fact long stretches of these roads were built by forced Tibetan labor and with the "loan" of vast quantities of grain and silver from the reserve granaries and treasury of the Government of Tibet. A Tibetan official has since computed that during four years of road construction—largely for Chinese military purposes—the Tibetans were required to "lend" the equivalent of nearly 10 million dollars in terms of grain and another 300,000 dollars in silver coinage. Working under conditions of extreme hardship comparable to those which attended the building of the Great Wall of China, thousands of Tibetans who were dragooned for this purpose paid with their lives, while others were subjected to much misery and suffering.

At the inaugural meeting of the Preparatory Committee in

Lhasa, the Panchen Lama was obsequious in his flattering references to the "achievements" of the Chinese Communists, but the Dalai Lama, while deferential, was obliquely critical. In a reference to the road construction program His Holiness mentioned "the many people who have sacrificed their valuable lives," and said, "I wish to express here my sincere condolence for the martyrs." He also referred pointedly to the indoctrination of the country's youth. "Several hundreds of the finest youths of the country," he remarked, had been sent by the Communists to study Marxism-Leninism in Peking's institutes for national minorities. "Tibet," said the Dalai Lama, "is the center of Lamaism. The whole population has a deep belief in Lamaism. The people treasure and protect their religious belief like their life. . . . Recently news from neighboring provinces and municipalities where reforms are being carried out or under preparation has reached Tibet and roused the suspicion and anxiety of some people here. . . . Tibet has no other alternative but to take the road of socialism. We must carry out reforms step by step." The statement was polite, but its implied note of protest and criticism could not have been lost on the Chinese.

In April, 1956, at the first meeting of the Preparatory Committee, the Chinese Vice Premier Chen Yi announced that "a railway from Lanchow to Lhasa will be built in the future." The Khamba uprising more than slightly dislocated this project, whose blueprint envisaged a rail line across the Chinghai Province area of Inner Tibet where in the Tsidam Basin, according to the Chinese Communists, potentially rich oilfields exist. On May 26, 1956, a Peking-Lhasa air-transport service on a ten-hour schedule was inaugurated, the first plane flying the new route being a Soviet IL-12.

What did this calculated opening of communications by land and air bring to the Tibetans? As a Tibetan refugee described it: "The first Chinese invaders proclaimed that they had come only to help the Tibetan people, not to interfere in their affairs, disturb their religion, or take anything from them—'not even needle or thread.' But they brought nothing with them but their mugs and their chopsticks, and the effect of their chopsticks and the effect of their inroads on essential supplies was to make prices rise by five or six times." The Tibetans had hoped that the opening of communications would ease many of their economic stresses and strains, as the Chinese had promised, but to their dismay these were increased.

"When the first vehicles began to arrive in 1953," said another Tibetan refugee, "they brought not more supplies but more and more Chinese. Prices rose still further."

Since the Chinese working personnel in Tibet "came only with their mugs and chopsticks," this was not surprising. The Dalai Lama himself drew the attention of the Preparatory Committee in 1957 to the growing inflationary trends, and mildly suggested that the administration had failed to notice the comparatively poor harvests turned out in many localities on account of drought. Therefore, it was difficult to reduce the prices of daily necessities when the prices of certain commodities, especially food and butter, "were gradually increasing." In fact, prices were mounting steeply.

The "difficulties" encountered in Tibet were confirmed by General Chang Ching-wu, Peking's chief representative in Tibet, in a speech to the State Council at Peking in 1955. "Owing to communications and transport difficulties and many other factors," he admitted, "what we have achieved is very little as far as the construction of Tibet and the consolidation of national defense are concerned. There have been grave misunderstandings among the nationalities. This, coupled with the unthorough education on the implementation of the Agreement of 1951, caused misunderstandings and doubts on the part of the Tibetan personnel, thus hindering the smooth progress of our work." It is odd that the Chinese, refusing to learn from experience, should repeat in Tibet the mistakes they made in China. To cite one instance: for the purpose of manufacturing steel in a primitive way the Communists in China proper mobilized some 50 million workers, building furnaces everywhere, regardless of communications and of the distance from the source of raw materials. According to a correspondent in the Yugoslav paper *Borba,* each of these 50 million workers manufactured at most two kilograms (4.4 pounds) of steel per day. Enormous quantities of ore, coal, coke, and metal scrap had to be transported, and suddenly there appeared the bottleneck: transportation.

In the year of "the great leap forward," the Communists in China intensified their land reforms by the introduction of communes, and by the end of December, 1958, there were a total of 26,000 communes in the country covering 99 per cent of China's peasant households. The primary aims of the communes are to step up agricultural production, overcome China's immediate labor shortage (due to lack of mechanical equipment), and curb the long-term problem of overpopulation. Yet during this year, to quote *Borba* again, there was stricter food rationing than before, and a concerted drive to limit consumption.

This experience has not deterred the Communist Chinese from introducing land reforms and attempting to establish communes in Tibet. That there was undoubtedly need for such reforms is widely acknowledged, and the Dalai Lama himself in his June 20th statement testified to the urgency for drastic changes in the prevailing system. "In particular," he declared, "it was my earnest desire that the system of land tenure should be radically changed without further delay and large landed estates [should be] acquired by the state on payment of compensation, for distribution amongst the tillers of the soil. But the Chinese authorities deliberately put every obstacle in the way of carrying out this just and reasonable reform. I desire to lay stress on the fact that we, as firm believers in Buddhism, welcome change and progress consistent with the genius of our people and the rich traditions of our country. But," His Holiness warned, "the people of Tibet will stoutly resist any victimization, sacrilege and plunder in the name of reforms, the policy which is now being enforced by representatives of the Chinese Government in Lhasa."

In the absence of statistics, the extent of the lands held by the monasteries, nobles, and other wealthy classes in Tibet cannot be accurately computed. Nor can their personal treasure in money, jewels, and other possessions be correctly estimated. But there is no denying that as Lamaism grew in influence the political importance and economic wealth of the monasteries expanded proportionately. The politico-religious domination of the lamas enabled them to achieve both power and privilege representing a vast vested interest steeped for the most part in archaic feudal customs. So also the rich nobility whose families are reckoned to number around two hundred. Tibet, in fact, is or rather was a medieval country with preponderating power and wealth in the hands of the church and the nobility. Yet its economic basis is agriculture and stockbreeding, with the tillers and the herdsmen as the chief props of this agricultural-pastoral society. Both these classes together constitute the largest numerical unit, enjoying no rights and certainly no riches.

Under the guise of introducing "democratic reforms," a comprehensive term for communization, the Chinese attempted to introduce a double-pronged program of land reforms and Han colonization in the border regions of Inner Tibet. The campaign was initiated in February, 1956, in western Szechwan, which contains a large number of Tibetans, but even earlier the Communists had imposed this socio-economic pattern in Inner Mongolia and Sikiang, both of which are officially "autonomous areas," a fact which throws a revealing light on what the Chinese mean by autonomy. In Inner Mongolia the Chinese outnumber the Mongols, as they do the Uighurs in Sinkiang. These moves created restiveness in the other minority regions, such as Szechwan, where the Khambas were in no mood to be clamped within a rigid superimposed mold.

There are some 60 national minorities in China occupying some 50 to 60 per cent of her total area, including regions rich in mineral resources; but their population, about 35 millions, is only about 6 per cent of the total. Although in theory they are guaranteed equal rights, in practice the key posts in the administration are held by Han cadres. "Without the help of the Han nationality and Han cadres, it is impossible to carry out Socialist reforms in the minority areas," a Chinese official statement proclaimed. From their own declarations the Chinese Communists in Tibet behaved like conquerors.

As a first step they ordered the formation of collective farms in the Kanze area of Szechwan province, transferring wholesale the farms, cattle, and sheep of the lamaseries and monasteries to "farm cooperatives." In April, 1956, Communist China's Vice Premier Chen Yi and General Chang Kuo-hua, addressing the Preparatory Committee, announced that "necessary reforms would be introduced to rid Tibet of its backward situation," adding arrogantly that this was also necessary to bring the Tibetans up to the level of "the advanced" Han nationality. Khamba repercussions were swift, and in June, 1956, the New China News Agency divulged that Jao Chia-tso, chairman of the Communist-controlled Chinese Buddhist Association, had informed the National People's Congress of rebellions on the eastern Tibetan border as a result of local dissatisfaction with Communist policies. Jao complained that "there were recently some improper measures on land reform, and commercial taxes on lamaseries, farmland, and cattle," and advised caution. For one thing, the lamas resented being asked to participate in agricultural cultivation, as this was contrary to traditional Buddhist regulations and customs. The conversion of their farmland and cattle into cooperatives deprived them of a major source of monastic revenue, while Chinese insistence that the lamas and monks should join in extirpating rats, birds, insects, and various types of vermin deeply offended their Buddhist susceptibilities, which regarded all forms of life as sacred. These "reforms" confirmed the suspicions of the lamas and their followers that the Chinese aimed at destroying the Buddhist religion.

The Khamba uprisings were concentrated in those regions where the "democratic reforms" were most widespread. These comprised the three autonomous areas of Liangshan, Apha, and Kanze, where some 4,800 agricultural cooperatives were set up with a total membership of 120,000 households, and which were the scene of rioting and rebellion from the opening months of 1956. Even before the Preparatory Committee held its inaugural meeting in April, reports of revolts in Tibet had reached Kalimpong and Khatmandu. Peking was forced to admit that guerrilla warfare was widespread in eastern and northeastern Tibet in the territories inhabited by the Khambas, Amdos, and Goloks. In the Batan-Litang area of Szechwan the Tibetans accused the Chinese of massacring over four thousand men, women, and children, bombing monasteries and other dwellings, and perpetrating cruelties on the local population. Within a few months the trouble had spilled across the Sino-Tibetan border into the Chamdo, Dinching, Nagchuka, and Loka areas of Tibet, where the rebels attacked agencies and army units of the Central People's Government. The uprisings compelled the Chinese Communists to revise their policies temporarily, and induced Mao Tse-tung to make his declaration of 1957, that the "democratic reforms" might be postponed until the third Five-Year Plan was inaugurated. In April this decision was formalized in a government decree.

But the Tibetans no longer respected the promises of the Communist Chinese, and were resentful of attempts at Han domination. As usual the Chinese and their henchmen attempted to explain away the uprisings as the work of feudal and religious reactionaries, the Panchen Lama denouncing the revolts as "the treacherous activities of the imperialists and separatists." On their part the leaders of the revolt made it clear that they were not opposed to land reforms, and in a declaration on January 1, 1959, proposed some radical changes in the social and political organizations of the country. These proposals included the acquisition of large landed estates on payment of compensation, the introduction of the elective system on the basis of adult suffrage, and the principle of individual liberty according to the accepted constitutional concept. The leaders of the revolt also declared: "We pledge ourselves for the improvement of the condition of our people and their standard of living. We engage ourselves to introduce all necessary reforms in the country in consonance with the natural conditions, customs, and genius of our people. In the field of economic development we pledge ourselves to improve the life of our nomadic people, of the tillers of the land, of the artisans and the handicraft men to the best of our ability and to effect changes in all by peaceful means." This declaration was supported not only by the masses but had the backing of the nobility, both lay and ecclesiastical. Certainly the tribesmen who spearheaded the revolt could hardly be described as members of the privileged classes.

The Tibetans were justified in their suspicion of Chinese

promises to go slow, for the Communist tactics were consistent with the doctrine which Mao propounded of letting
a hundred flowers bloom, a device to trap those opposed to
the Red ideologies to come out and expose themselves. The
flowers soon turned to weeds, and the Chinese then got down
to the job of uprooting them. Late in 1957 the Central Committee of the Chinese Communist party dispatched a five-
man mission to Lhasa for "weeding out reactionaries" who
"come in the way of modernizing Tibet on socialistic lines."
Peking thereafter prepared to get tough.

The Chinese infiltration tactics were resumed, and pursued
several courses, and these in turn provoked Tibetan resistance
which culminated in the revolution spreading to Lhasa and
in the flight of the Dalai Lama. In September and October,
1958, the Communists launched a campaign in Chinghai and
Kansu having as its obvious purpose the destruction of the
Buddhist religion, which the Chinese sought to undermine
by labeling the lamas as oppressors of the masses. Undoubtedly many of Tibet's religious fraternity are noted for their
rapacity. But the age-long attachment of the Tibetans to
Lamaism, to reverence for the Buddha and for traditional
values asserted itself against the Communists. The failure of
the Chinese to rouse the Tibetan masses against the lamas
was demonstrated when the Communists were driven to play
even the nomadic herdsmen against each other by placing
"reactionary herd owners" in the same category as the lamas
and inviting the masses to attack both. With few exceptions
these ignorant, illiterate, and landless people did neither, for
even to their unlettered minds the Chinese attack seemed to
be an offensive against religion, not against privilege.

Han chauvinism, though deprecated officially by word of
mouth, then began to be implemented by deed. In 1956 General Chang Kuo-hua had mildly warned the Tibetans that
an influx of Chinese settlers was imminent and had implied

that these immigrants would help to advance the country's economy more rapidly. The two major highways from Tibet to China had been completed the year before, and a trickle of Han immigrants had begun to seep in since then. In 1958 this trickle assumed menacing proportions as masses of Chinese youths descended on the country. Although the Peking press described their reception in Tibet as enthusiastic and friendly, one report claiming that the Tibetans had warmly welcomed the Hans "in a manner in which they might celebrate their own festivals" and that the Tibetans and Chinese had "told one another about their own customs and exchanged production experience," the actual Tibetan reaction was neither friendly nor enthusiastic. Peking had inspired this fresh drive for mass Chinese settlement in Tibet, and this is borne out by Marshal Chu Teh's appeal in December, 1958, to the youth of China to go and colonize the "frontier areas"—a modern and Eastern variant of "Go west, young man."

The Chinese immigrants settled largely in the populous and arable regions of eastern Tibet, particularly in the Kham and Amdo districts. Their number * is not known but it was enough to alarm the frontier Tibetans, who are mostly tribesmen, and to unite them in a common front against this alien influx. The Chinese sense of superiority vis-à-vis the Tibetans aggravated the latter's hostility. "Part of the Han cadres," noted the Peking Government representative in a report to the Chinese State Council, "have demonstrated a varying degree of the remnant concept of Great Hanism, such as lack of due respect to the religious beliefs, customs, and habits of the Tibetans, the insufficient recognition of the merits of the Tibetan cadres, and the lack of due respect and warm support of them." Even so pronounced a Tibetan collaborator as

* One estimate gives it at 500,000, but no authentic figures are available. Another estimate places the total at 5,000,000.

Ngabon Ngawang Jigme observed that "in individual cases some Chinese Communist cadres and Chinese army officers and soldiers, owing to ignorance of Tibetan customs and habits and because of language difficulties, occasionally committed defects and errors in trading and transport work in certain districts."

Apart from the fear of being swamped by the Chinese inflow, the Tibetans were disturbed by its economic consequences and by the impact on their religious traditions of the Communist infiltration. "The economic effect of the 'liberation' of Tibet," stated Thubten Nyenjik, former abbot of Gyantse monastery who was also governor of Gyantse Province and is now a refugee in India, "has been disastrous. Before the advent of the Chinese the economy of Tibet was sound, the cost of living low, and the Tibetan Government was in a position to aid its people in their economic, social, cultural, and religious aspirations. But now, owing to the influx of 100,000 Chinese soldiers who live off the Tibetans, their granaries are empty, for the Chinese take 'loans' which are never repaid; the vast herds of yaks and flocks of sheep have been decimated, trees in government- and private-owned parks uprooted for firewood, and the economy of the country has been so disrupted that the cost of living for the bare necessities of life has risen nine and ten times, and where formerly there was a large exportable surplus, these commodities have now to be imported." Thubten Nyenjik also warned that, despite Communist talk of autonomy, the Chinese "are committed to the obliteration of the religion, culture, and tradition of a non-Chinese people so that the people might become indistinguishable from the millions of Chinese. . . . Such is the meaning of Chinese autonomy for Tibet."

Parenthetically it might be noted that during the past three years some 1,380,000 Han people have migrated to northeast and northwest China and Inner Mongolia. Peking decided, in November, 1958, to transfer more Chinese manpower to the Ninghsia region, where one-third of the population is already of Han stock. In this Moslem region the China Association for the Promotion of Moslem Culture was by a curious coincidence concluded during the same month. The Chinese explain this mass migration by claiming that it satisfies the demand of the various nationalities for help in construction work over the next few years. But the Tibetan reaction, as well as the repercussions in other minority areas, does not endorse this interpretation. The real reason animating Communist policy is revealed in a Chinese statement: "The question of whether or not to accept the Han cadres and immigrants is precisely also the question of whether or not to accept Socialism."

In other minor ways the Chinese Communists have also sought to harass the Tibetans into subservience. Under the 1951 agreement the Tibetan Government had agreed actively to "assist the People's Liberation Army to enter Tibet and consolidate the national defense." It had, moreover, consented to the Chinese demand that the Tibetan troops would be "reorganized" by stages and become a part of the national defense forces of the People's Republic of China. The Tibet Military Area Headquarters of the Chinese Army was established, as noted, in February, 1952, and almost immediately efforts were made by the Chinese to undermine the loyalty of Tibetan officers and soldiers. Since Tibet was virtually governed by the PLA Tibetan Military District Command, this presented few difficulties; but it is eloquent of the average Tibetan's antipathy to the Han intruder that the loyalty of very few Tibetan soldiers was suborned.

The indoctrination of the armed forces proceeded alongside that of the civilian population. Like other Tibetans, they were inundated with Communist propaganda through posters, pamphlets, lectures, and study classes but proved equally impervious and immune. Including the Dalai Lama's personal bodyguard of 5,000 soldiers, the Tibetan armed forces numbered around 10,000, and it is significant of the failure of the Chinese Communists to undermine their loyalty that the army took a prominent part in the revolt against the invaders. The first local congress of the Chinese Communist party was held in Lhasa in December, 1952, and was attended by nearly 340 delegates representing party members in the various units of the Tibetan military command. It was reported here that over four hundred Tibetans had been trained by PLA units in the school set up for this purpose. Three years later the State Council at Peking decided "to expand and strengthen" the Tibetan Military District Cadres School, changing its name to Cadres School for the Tibet Area. The same meeting of the State Council, on the initiative of Ngabon Ngawang Jigme, considered a "request" by the Tibetan Government for help in reorganizing the Tibetan Army and redeeming the Tibetan currency.

Although a great deal of trade inside Tibet is by barter, the country has its own currency, with the *sang* as the monetary unit. Until the Chinese came, Indian rupees circulated freely inside Tibet, but the Communists have succeeded in largely replacing these, as well as Tibetan coinage, by Chinese currency. Shortly after the flight of the Dalai Lama Indian currency was not allowed to circulate in the country. Tibet had also its postal system, and the Dalai Lama's government issued its own postage stamps. Until about two years ago the Government of India arranged for the carriage of mail from Lhasa to the outside world through Gyantse, but the mail is now routed north and east through China to foreign lands. Chinese postage stamps are gradually replacing the Tibetan.

So Tibet, whose previous window on the world was mainly

India, is being reoriented toward China, and taught to regard herself as part of the great motherland of the Han world. Pressures and pinpricks are collectively and cumulatively being applied to force her into the Communist mold. The greatest of these pressures is the Chinese effort to destroy the power of the lamas, undermine Buddhism, and substitute the supremacy of Communism. But of all pressures the Tibetans are most antipathetic to this one, for from time immemorial Tibet has been the Land of Lamas.

land
of
lamas

CHAPTER FOUR

In the theocratic society of Tibet, as we have seen, the lamas constituted the predominant class not only concerned with their ecclesiastical duties but also participating in trade and sharing in the work of government, civilian, and military as well. Their power, before the Chinese Communists took over, was pervasive, their wealth immense and immeasurable. They were indeed a caste apart, for only through them could the ordinary person approach the gods of the Lamaist pantheon. Tibet was a country ruled by priests.

We have noted how Lamaism evolved as a mixture of Bon, the ancient Tibetan animistic religion, Buddhism, and certain Hindu practices of the Tantric type. The Tantras, the sacred books of the cult of Siva,* date from the sixth and seventh centuries of the Christian era, and consist of dialogues between Siva and his *Shakti,* or Female Energy, one

* One of the gods of the Hindu Triad representing destruction and creation.

of whose names is Durga (The Inaccessible). A shakti is usually depicted in a carnal embrace with the god who generated her. While the male divinity represents *karuna* (compassion) the female embodies *prajna* (perfect knowledge), which suggests a certain equality of the sexes.

Buddhism has gone through three main evolutions since Gautama first preached it six centuries before Christ. In their pristine form the Buddha's teachings and monastic rules are contained in the *Tripitka* written in Pali by the early Buddhists of South India and Ceylon. *Tripitka* means "three baskets," and these are the *Vinaya,* which deals with monastic rules; the *Sutra,* the repository of the doctrine of the Buddha; and the *Abhidhamma,* which contains the metaphysical and philosophical discussions on Buddhist doctrine.

The gist of Gautama's teaching is to be found in the Four Noble Truths and the Noble Eightfold Path which the Buddha discovered while meditating under a pipal tree and which he first proclaimed to his five companions in the Park of the Gazelles at Banaras. To them he expounded the Four Noble Truths and showed how they led to the Noble Eightfold Path:

"Now this, monks, is the noble truth of pain: birth is painful, old age is painful, sickness is painful, death is painful, sorrow, lamentation, dejection and despair are painful. Contact with unpleasant things is painful, not getting what one wishes is painful. . . .

"Now this, monks, is the noble truth of the cause of pain: the craving which tends to rebirth, combined with pleasure and lust, finding pleasure here and there, namely the craving for passion, the craving for existence, the craving for non-existence.

"Now this, monks, is the noble truth of the cessation of pain, the cessation without a remainder of craving, the abandonment, forsaking, release, non-attachment.

"Now this, monks, is the noble truth of the way that leads to the cessation of pain: this is the noble Eightfold Way, namely right views, right intention, right speech, right action, right livelihood, right effort, right mindedness, right concentration.

"This is the noble truth of pain: Thus, monks, among doctrines unheard before, in me sight and knowledge arose, wisdom arose, knowledge arose, light arose." *

With the Buddha's death his teachings took various forms, according to the interpretations of his disciples and followers. Attempts were made to resolve controversial points, and at least three councils were summoned for this purpose but with no positive result. In time the original philosophy evolved into a religion with the Buddha elevated to the status of a deity. Buddhism reached its apogee in India in the reign of the great emperor-apostle Asoka in the third century B.C.

Thereafter it went through several vicissitudes, moving away from Gautama's agnosticism to a sort of metaphysical polytheism, dividing finally into two schools—the Hinayana or Theravada, which survives in Ceylon and is faithful to the Buddha's original doctrine; and the Mahayana, polytheistic and metaphysical, where each individual trains himself to become a Buddha, being known in the process of attainment as a Bodhisattva, that is, a being destined for enlightenment, who deliberately renounces nirvana, the state of ultimate bliss, to remain among his fellow men and serve them. The Mahayana school flourishes in Tibet and Japan, and was once active in China.

In Tibet, Buddhism took the form of Lamaism with, as we noted, the animistic elements of Bon and the Tantric practices of Hinduism grafted onto it. This type of Buddhism is known as Vajrayana, the Buddhism of the Adamantine

---

* Edward J. Thomas's translation in *Early Buddhist Scriptures* (Routledge & Kegan Paul, Ltd., 1935).

Vehicle, with a strong belief in reincarnation, and influenced by demonology.

Like Buddhism, which in time was divided into sects, Lamaism also took various forms—the Kadampa, or Red Hats, established by Atisha; the Gelugpa, or Yellow Hats, the predominant sect, to which the Dalai Lama and the Panchen Lama belong; and various other sects—the Sagya, or Colored, sect, founded by Basba, tutor of Kublai Khan, which established the lay-ecclesiastical system of government; and the Kargyupa, or White, sect founded by Marpa, the guru of Milarepa, the hermit-philosopher of eleventh century Tibet.

Lamaism has an extensive literature contained in the 108 volumes of the *Kangyur,* which comprises the scripture of Tibetan Buddhism, including the *Vinaya,* or canon law, and the 225 volumes of the *Tangyur,* which consists of commentaries on the scriptures. Although the larger monasteries in Tibet grant degrees in divinity, the scholarship is said to be of a not very high order. The highest intellectual of the Lamaist church is the Ganden Dzeba, the Enthroned of Ganden monastery, who holds his office for seven years, and whose mastery of philosophy and religious knowledge entitles him to sit in the seat of the great Tsong Ka-pa, founder of the Yellow sect. During the New Year even the Dalai Lama had to bow to the Enthroned. Succession at the end of the Ganden Dzeba's seven-year term was determined by examination, this being conducted by the Dalai and Panchen lamas and by the monk vacating the seat.

Head of the religious hierarchy was the Dalai Lama, who was also the supreme secular power, with the Panchen Lama exercising only spiritual authority until the advent of the Chinese. The local Tibetan Government headed by the Dalai Lama had its seat in Lhasa, and His Holiness's direct authority extended over U, the largest single area of Tibet, comprising nearly 110 dzongs, or counties. The Panchen

Lama's authority was confined to the much smaller area of Tsang, and even here a number of counties were controlled by the Dalai Lama's followers and by adherents of the Sagya, or Colored, sect.

Ranking below the two Grand Lamas were the Incarnate Lamas, numbering about one thousand, and headed by the abbots of the Three Great monasteries of Drepung, Sera, and Ganden, all situated in the vicinity of Lhasa. The Dalai Lama studied at these centers until he was installed on the Golden Throne, and the abbots of these monasteries wielded great spiritual and political power. Drepung, some six miles west of Lhasa at the foot of the hills which flank the plain on the north, is one of the largest monasteries in the world, housing around ten thousand inmates. Sera, three miles north of the capital, has a temple dedicated to Dorje-chang, also known as Vajradhara; while Ganden, some twenty-five miles east of Lhasa, is the oldest monastery of the Yellow sect, having been founded by Tsong Ka-pa, who was its first abbot. From the "Big Three" came the majority of monk-officials and high ecclesiastics. The Incarnate Buddhas are trained at these centers.

Tibet is studded with about three thousand monasteries, but the vast majority are small local monasteries and hermitages with often less than one hundred inmates, though some of the bigger ones house as many as one thousand or more. Besides the Big Three there are other well-known monasteries, or *gompas,* as the Tibetans call them. These include the monastery at Samye, about forty miles from Lhasa, which was once used as a government treasury; Tholing, Tsaparang, and Kochar in western Tibet; and many others spread throughout the country. Nuns and nunneries are also numerous, but they occupy an inferior place despite the Tantric doctrine, since women are not deemed the spiritual equals of men. Other centers of religion are the temples.

Among the better known are the Jokhang and Ramoche in Lhasa and the Kumbum at Gyantse, which has been described as the Assisi of Mahayana Buddhism. Dominating Lhasa are the golden roofs and sloping walls of the Potala, winter residence of the Dalai Lama, which at one time housed a veritable army of monks and retainers. In the center of the Potala is the Red Palace containing the principal halls, chapels, and shrines of past Dalai Lamas. Here also are life-sized effigies of Song-tsan Gampo and of his two wives. The Potala hill on which stands the palace of the Dalai Lama is named after a hill at Cape Comorin in South India. There is a third Potala, a hill on the coast of the Chinese mainland.

The Lamaist hierarchy has similarities with that of the Roman Catholic Church, the Dalai Lama being for all practical purposes the Pope of Lamaism. Below him and the Panchen Lama are the abbots of the great monasteries, known as *chutuktus,* whose status corresponds in many respects to that of the Roman cardinals. Like the two Grand Lamas, they bear the title of Rimpoche, or Glorious. Next in order of gradation are the *chubilkans,* who are abbots of the lesser monasteries, and, like the chutuktus, they are regarded as Incarnate Lamas. A number of monasteries in Tibet contain one or more of these Incarnate Lamas.

Aside from the Incarnate Lamas there are ordinary lamas, whose number runs into thousands and who are distinguished from the monks by their learning of the Tibetan scriptures and by the practice of meditation and penance. The junior monks are known as *dabas* or *trapas,* and sometimes function in a servile capacity to the lamas as servants. The ordinary lamas hold various ranks and degrees corresponding roughly to the Western hierarchy of deacon, priest, dean, and doctor of divinity. The larger monasteries are theological colleges, but the Big Three alone confer the coveted degree of

Ge Shi (Devoted to Virtue) on the lamas who have mastered scriptural and other esoteric studies. Of the Ge Shi lamas a small number are chosen to enter one of the two academies attached to the Ganden monastery. These are the Gyu-Me and Gyu-To academies, which specialize in advanced studies in Tantric Lamaism. Ultimately, as noted before, the most learned scholar and master of religious theory, as well as of esoteric practices, is installed as the Enthroned at Ganden with the title of Ganden Dzeba, the office originally occupied by Tsong Ka-pa. Until the Dalai Lama left Tibet, the abbots of Drepung, Sera, and Ganden, along with eight government officials, presided over the Tsongdu, or National Assembly. No decision was taken without the assent of the clerics.

Those who aspire to priesthood in Tibet generally enter a monastery around the age of eight, though there have been entrants aged only four. Here the candidate lives a life of strict discipline, celibacy, and abstinence enforced more often than not by the whip. Whereas the Dalai and Panchen lamas invariably come from poor families, the status of an acolyte or monk inside a monastery is often determined by his wealth, and wealthy monks have houses of their own inside the monastery, do no menial work, and have their food prepared for them. Some among those from poor families are able in time to read and write and advance in the monastic hierarchy, but the majority are condemned to work for the greater part of their lives as servants catering to the needs of the more affluent monks. These serving monks are known as monk-servants. A monk is allowed to sow seed but not to dig or plow, which again places the poor monks at a disadvantage, for they cannot afford to pay their lay tenants to till the soil. On the other hand they can engage in trade, and to be a monk, whether one is the son of a peasant or herdsman, is to enjoy a status superior to that of the laity.

A candidate for priesthood passes through three stages before he becomes a fully ordained monk. He begins as a pupil probationer or *ge-nyen,* advances to be a novice or *get-isul,* and finally is graduated as a fully ordained monk or *ge-long.* As a Buddhist monk he is required to observe no less than some 250 vows, and there are said to be fifteen ways of approaching nirvana after overcoming the 84,000 human passions which in the Lamaist vocabulary afflict mankind.

Over the centuries a vast mass of wealth in the form of gold, treasure, and land has congealed in the vaults and records of these monasteries which without exception possess land and engage in trade. One estimate reckons that collectively the monasteries of Tibet own a third of the country's arable lands. These lands are worked by serfs, who earn no wages but are paid in kind, in the form of food grains and crops according to a tariff arbitrarily fixed by the lamas or landlords. The higher rank of monks augment their income from trade, rent, and moneylending, with presents, monetary and material, for officiating at marriages, births, deaths, festivals, and in sickness.

Undoubtedly lamaism meant lucrative living. According to Heinrich Harrer, who spent seven years in Tibet,* during one month a monastery in Lhasa received from the government three tons of tea and fifty tons of butter in addition to subsidies totaling over 100,000 dollars. Liberal gifts of *tsamba,* a flour of baked barley or wheat, which the Tibetans usually knead with their butter-tea, are not uncommon.

In their campaign to undermine Lamaism and finally to uproot it, the Communists have been following in Tibet the same tactics they employed against the Buddhists in China. According to the Chinese the number of Buddhist monks and nuns in China, including Tibet, is roughly 500,000, while the number of Buddhist followers totals 100 million. Of the 500,000, about 200,000 monks reside in Tibet proper, while

* *Seven Years in Tibet* (New York: E. P. Dutton & Company, Inc., 1954).

another 100,000 live in the Tibetan-populated areas of Chinghai, Szechwan, and Kansu. In Inner Mongolia there are 20,000. This leaves a balance of 180,000 Buddhist monks in China proper. Before the Communists seized power, there were 700,000.

"Followers of Marxism-Leninism are from top to bottom atheists," declared the People's Daily, official organ of the Chinese Communist party in November, 1951. In the Communist view, religion, as Marx propounded, is the opium of the people, lulling them into docility and meek acquiescence with their way of life. If the Communists make a show of religious tolerance, it is only to achieve their ultimate political ends. In his book Principles of New Democracy, Mao Tse-tung indicates how religion can be exploited for this purpose. "Communist party members," he explains, "may very well form an anti-imperialist united battlefront in political activities with certain proponents of idealism, and even with religionists, but they should never agree with their idealism or their religious doctrines."

In China, as later in Tibet and other "national minority areas," the Communists mounted their offensive against religion under various guises. Although in China as in Tibet they first made a show of tolerance and even of appeasement, it was not long before they made their real purpose plain. In October, 1948, a year before they officially assumed power, the Central China Bureau of the Chinese Communist party announced a set of regulations called "Principles Governing Rental and Interest Reductions" whereunder they promised that "land owned by religious bodies shall remain untouched. If it is not being administered by any special body, it shall come under the provisions governing disposal of land belonging to runaway landlords. Land belonging to runaway landlords shall be placed under the custody of their relatives. If there are no relatives the Government will take custody."

These promises and provisos seemed reasonable enough in theory but were far different in practice. The Agrarian Reform Law of 1949 contained an article abolishing ownership rights of religious bodies, temples, monasteries, and churches, though no drastic efforts were immediately made to implement the policy. The official line was still to appease Buddhism, thereby lulling the fear and suspicions of indigenous Buddhists and simultaneously gaining the good will of Buddhists abroad. By 1951 the Red regime in China had begun to stabilize itself, and the Communists then shifted cautiously to the attack, working largely through their front, the so-called Chinese Buddhist Association founded in June, 1953, which initially had only two branches—one significantly in Tibet and the other in the Thai-Chingpo autonomous *chou,* or district, of Yunnan. Other branches were established later in Inner Mongolia, Kansu, Shansi, Liasoning, the Sibsong-Pana autonomous chou in Yunnan, and the Apha-Tibetan autonomous chou in Szechwan.

Behind this front the Chinese Communists sought to discredit Buddhism under cover of land reform, accusing Buddhism of "serving the purpose of feudalism," and labeling the Buddhist clergy as "lackeys of the exploiting class." A Central Government decree of August 4, 1950, classified monks and nuns, both Buddhist and Taoist,* along with geomancers, fortunetellers, diviners, and superstitious practitioners. Since in China as in Tibet the monasteries undoubtedly owned extensive properties, and since religious custom ordained that the Buddhist clergy could not till the soil themselves, they proved an easy target for the Commu-

---

* Taoism is a religion of China founded by Lao Tzu in the sixth century B.C.

nists. Head monks or abbots were particularly denounced as "feudalistic landlords who depend for a living on the blood and sweat of the working people, not working themselves but living on the spoils of their exploitation."

Through the Chinese Buddhist Association the Communists thereupon set out to "reform" the clergy whose property holdings of temples and monasteries, with a few exceptions for show purposes, had already been confiscated. They did this by emphasizing three themes. First, all Chinese Buddhist monks and nuns were called upon to accept the leadership of the Communist party and resolutely take the road to Socialism. This meant, in the words of Ulanfu, chairman of the Inner Mongolia Autonomous Region, that the lamas must "either join a cooperative or operate a joint public-private stock farm." They have in fact been dragooned into doing so, and in one cooperative in Inner Mongolia every lama is required to do 260 days of work a year, which, though permitted by a few Buddhist sects such as the Zen, leave the average monk after attending the "thought reform" or "brainwashing" classes very little time to perform his religious duties. The compulsion to undergo ideological remolding constitutes the second major theme, the two being sometimes lumped under the composite head of "the movement of productive labor and study." The third major theme is the necessity for all the clergy to "draw a clear line of demarcation between the enemy and themselves" and "to expose bad men and bad things to the government." Not only are Buddhists set against Buddhists but they are also set against the Taoists. In March, 1958, a meeting of Buddhists in Kiangsi pledged to "fight to the end against reactionary Taoist sects." Similarly Chinese Moslem imams or priests and Mongolian lamas have since early 1950 been the especial objects of Communist-inspired denunciations. Like the old landowners in China, religious leaders in Tibet and other national minority areas are put on platforms and the masses are invited and incited to accuse and denounce them.

The Chinese have began to adopt these tactics in Tibet. There, as in China, the lamas are being "persuaded" to work rather than pray, to earn rather than beg, and to participate in the world rather than reject it. Such compulsory participation often takes strange forms. In November, 1958, Shirob Jaltso, chairman of the Buddhist Association in Chinghai, declared in a speech to a group of Tibetans that "the killing of rats and locusts is compatible with our religion. We kill not only locusts but also any other harmful elements such as imperialists and counterrevolutionaries." The first rule of the *Vinaya* ordains that a Buddhist shall not take the life of any sentient being. Around this time a meeting of Tibetan monks in Chinghai was called upon to shout, "American troops, get out of Lebanon!" The Buddhist Association, one of whose honorary presidents was the Dalai Lama, was used to bolster up the Communist peace front, and Buddhist monks from China and Tibet were prominent among the delegates to the conference of World Peace Supporters held in Tokyo in April, 1954.

Chinese pressure on the lamas in Tibet proper was at first cautious. Even in the border areas such as Chinghai the drive against the monasteries was calculatedly moderate in its tempo, and for some time the lamaseries there continued to receive their original rents from peasant villages even after these had been made cooperatives. Only in 1958 when the Khambas in western Szechwan stepped up their resistance did the Chinese Communists clamp down on the rebels and direct a fierce offensive against the monasteries.

In Tibet proper, the Chinese, realizing that Lamaism had its roots in the people, proceeded slowly. "Members of the Tibetan race, be they roving herdsmen or agriculturists, are all believers in Lamaism," the Peking *Kwang Ming Daily*

News acknowledged. "Tibet's rulers therefore utilize Lama-ism to intoxicate the general populace and as a means of support for their measures of domination and exploitation." But the Chinese Reds were themselves not averse to exploiting religion. Aware of the wide geographical distribution of Buddhism in countries and states such as Burma, Ceylon, Viet Nam, Thailand, Bhutan, Sikkim, and Nepal, the Communists behind a show of respect for religion set about utilizing it politically. They pursued this policy with characteristic cynicism, and while respectfully welcoming the Dalai and Panchen lamas and several of the Incarnate Lamas from Tibet they had no compunction in ravaging famous centers of worship such as the Ta Euh temple in Chinghai and requisitioning the Chin Yah temple (The Temple of Golden Tiles) to house the Military and Political Institute of Chinghai Province. Nor did Communist vandalism stop there. Images of the Buddha, bronze figures, and holy relics taken from temples and monasteries were sent abroad to other countries, including the Soviet Union. Sometimes this was done as a political stunt. Thus a tooth of the Buddha was loaned to Burma in 1955–1956 while the bones of the scholar-pilgrim Hsuan Tsang were dispatched to the Nalanda Institute in India. Another of Hsuan Tsang's bones was presented to the Buddhists of Ceylon, and in Japan the Chinese Buddhist Association sponsored a monthly magazine from June, 1957, entitled *Japanese and Chinese Buddhism*.

When the Chinese Communists ventured on the "peaceful occupation" of Tibet in October, 1950, the Northwest China Administrative Council made a formal announcement "exempting land owned by the monasteries of Lamaism from requisition and distribution"; but, as General Chang Kuo-hua later explained, freedom of religious belief was not to be confused with freedom of counterrevolutionary activities carried out by "bandits under red robes." Nonetheless soon after the occupation of Tibet the Chinese Communists attempted to bring the lamas into line, but met with strong resistance. Not only the monasteries but the people at large resisted measures such as the formation of cooperatives and the enforcement of agricultural cultivation by the monks. The opposition was so widespread and firm that the Communists had to beat a retreat, and in April, 1957, they formally postponed, as we noted, their "democratic reforms" until after 1962. At the Eighth Congress of the Chinese Communist party in Peking in September, 1956, Liu Shao-chi, the party theoretician who was then vice chairman of the Politburo, advised: "In regard to religious belief in the areas of national minorities, we must *for some time* adhere to the policy of freedom of religious belief and must never interfere in that connection during social reform." In other words, the Chinese Communists were counseled to bide their time.

They had not very long to wait, for by March, 1959, the train of rebellion lighted by the Khambas in western Szechwan as far back as December, 1955, exploded in Lhasa with the flight of the Dalai Lama. After that the Communists had no need even for pretense. The crushing of the rebellion in Lhasa by March 22nd—though it still continues in the outlying northern and eastern regions—was followed less than a week later by Peking's peremptory dissolution of the Dalai Lama's local Government of Tibet on March 28th and the declaration that the Preparatory Committee set up in 1956 for the proposed Tibetan Autonomous Region should "exercise the functions and powers of the local Tibet Government." The Dalai Lama's supporters on the Preparatory Committee, who numbered eighteen, were summarily dismissed and replaced by sixteen supporters of the Panchen Lama, who was appointed acting chairman of the committee, the Dalai Lama still being nominally permitted to retain the chairmanship of that body. The Chinese action had a double motivation. In the first place, by keeping the chairmanship open to the Dalai Lama the Communists, flourishing an olive branch, probably still hoped to inveigle him back. Second, Tibetan tradition ordains that if the Dalai Lama happens, for whatever reason, to be incapacitated the Panchen Lama can assume neither the God-king's secular nor his religious authority. In the prevailing circumstances the Chinese had to make a show of respecting indigenous custom.

However, there was no longer any need for Peking to pretend that its authority was other than omnipotent in Tibet. An official news agency comment flatly announced that "until further notice" Chinese Communist troops would control all religious, social, and governmental functions in Tibet. The Chinese openly abandoned their policy of "gradualism." Among the first acts of the new Preparatory Committee was the administrative redivision of Tibet from five into seven zones, designed, as was frankly announced, to erase the "old feudalistic carving up of land" between the lamas, the nobility, and the traders. The Tibet Autonomous Area now consists of seven Zones—Shigatse, Chamdo, Takun, Loka, Gyantse, Tsangchuka, and Ari, with Lhasa, seat of the Dalai Lama, converted into a municipality. For all practical purposes the Dalai Lama has been written off, and along with him the lamas and nobility, as well as the official hierarchy of the chi-kyap and the dzongpons. Evidently the Chinese aim at substituting for them in Tibet the so-called official cadres of glorified clerks recruited largely from the rural areas, such as exist in China.

That the Tibetan rebellion still continues is obvious from the order of priorities listed by the Chinese Communists and their creatures in Tibet. According to the Panchen Lama and General Chang Kuo-hua, both of whom addressed the second plenary session of the Preparatory Committee in July, 1959, at Lhasa, the first task was to suppress the rebellion and the second to introduce "democratic reforms." What shape these would take was indicated in some detail.

"A campaign," said General Chang, "will be carried out in the monasteries and temples to oppose rebellion, privileges, and exploitation. At the same time," he continued blandly, "the policy of the Communist party and the government of the freedom of religious belief will be firmly adhered to." He termed redistribution of land the second stage of Tibetan reform under the Communists, when the old order would be abolished and "peasants' associations" would be established. These associations would become the basic form of mass leadership and would exercise the functions and power of the government "at basic levels," a clue to what the administrative redivision portends.

The Panchen Lama dutifully endorsed the general's remarks, adding more specifically that "temples and monasteries will inevitably be involved during the reform since the temples and monasteries and some of the high-ranking lamas in them possess manorial estates and are serf owners.* It will not be beneficial to religion if the serfs of the aristocratic feudal government are emancipated while the serfs of the lamaseries are to remain in bondage. Genuine and philanthropic religion must not retain any stigma of serfdom. Therefore, many feudal systems of oppression and exploitation existing in the lamaseries should also be reformed." In

* This seems highly ironic in the context of the description of the Panchen Lama's palace at Shigatse by the pro-Communist Alan Winnington in his book *Tibet* (Lawrence & Wishart, London, 1957). Winnington describes the Tashi-lhunpo monastery where the Panchen Lama resides in the following terms: "A greater sense of wealth and pomp pervades the Tashi-lhunpo monastery, winter home of the Panchen Lama, than any single monastery in Lhasa. The biggest pieces of turquoise I ever saw are let in as floor slabs before some of the altars."

the light of Winnington's observations, reform might appropriately begin with the Tashi-lhunpo monastery of the Panchen Lama.

Both the Panchen Lama and General Chang Kuo-hua warned the Tibetan "rebels" who had been loyal to the Dalai Lama that they would be punished in various ways, including the confiscation of all their lands and properties. This is now being done. On the other hand, in accordance with the traditional Marxist tactics, "collaborators" in the landlord class who took no part in the rebellion were promised that they would be treated "with consideration." Their lands, livestock, and property holdings in excess of the maximum allowed under the property redistribution plan would be paid for in full by the government—naturally according to the government's assessment. "Those," said the Panchen Lama, "who have used the land to exploit the broad masses of the people for centuries and thus become debtors of the people should, as a matter of course, return the land to the people without receiving any compensation." Who these "debtors of the people" are would again naturally be determined by the government.

The Panchen Lama, echoing his master's voice, announced that the policy of "buying out" landowners would also be adopted toward "the upper strata members who have not taken part in the rebellion." As a general rule, he added, herds would not be redistributed except in the case of "rebel" owners. Livestock under such ownership would be handed to herdsmen who had not opposed the Chinese.

How did the Communists redeem these equivocal promises? In Inner Mongolia and the border areas, as noted, they had bunched together "reactionary herd owners and lamas" in an attempt to identify one with the other, and to turn the more indigent monks and herdsmen against both. In Tibet itself, along with the herd owners, the more affluent lamas were obliged to appear on public platforms where they were made the targets of an "antifeudal complaints struggle." Unfortunately for the Communists, the masses displayed no great enthusiasm for this campaign, which led the Chinese to accuse "the reactionary clique of the upper strata in Tibet" of ignoring "the interests of the broad masses of the people, ecclesiastical and secular." It is not that "the broad masses" did not want reforms. They were eager for them, but the methods adopted by the Communists to enforce these reforms seemed to the ordinary Tibetan calculated attempts by the Han foreigners to undermine their religion and destroy their traditions.

On March 31, 1959, about a fortnight after the Dalai Lama had left Lhasa and three days after the local Tibetan Government was dissolved, the Peking *People's Daily* suggested in an editorial that the rebellion "has proved the necessity of instituting democratic reforms." The Reds were preparing to apply to Tibet the ideological pattern they had tried to impose in Szechwan and Chinghai. "How long can the lamas remain privileged in Tibet while they are reformed in Chinghai?" the Communists demanded. As far back as October, 1956, the Reds had forced the establishment in Tibet of the Buddhist Association which had been launched in China three years before. But Tibetan non-cooperation rendered this organization more or less quiescent. The Chinese complained that their efforts were being nullified by the "idealism-theism" of the Tibetan masses, and the *Kuang Ming Daily News* was moved later to confess, "We dared not publicize materialism and atheism out of fear that this would come in conflict with religious policy and arouse the apprehensions of the masses."

With the departure of the Dalai Lama and the installation of the Panchen Lama in political authority, Peking set out to institute its land reforms in Tibet on the lines followed by the Communists in China from 1949 to 1951. First, peasants' associations were formed to exercise governmental powers on the village level, this "reform" following almost automatically the elimination of the chi-kyaps and dzongpons. Among the duties of these associations is the task of seeing that land is given only to those who are politically reliable. In the pastoral area herds belonging to Tibetan rebels were confiscated, and since a large percentage of herdsmen took part in the revolt this policy gave the Communists wide scope to eliminate political opposition.

In Chinghai, Szechwan, and other parts of Communist China inhabited by Tibetans, "democratic reforms" had included confiscation of herds, the formation of communes, and campaigns intended to reduce popular respect for Tibetan monks and the Buddhist religion. These "democratic reforms" were now promulgated in Tibet proper, where the Chinese got the Panchen Lama to declare that "feudal oppression and exploitation in monasteries would be abolished." The Panchen Lama had been summoned to Peking early in April, 1959, soon after the Preparatory Committee was designated Tibet's new local administration, and remained in China until late June.

"Struggle meetings" were organized on a wide scale throughout Tibet where the lamas were charged with charlatanism, robbery, torture, fraud, and all manner of misdemeanors. Since the monasteries were large landowners these "struggle meetings," while utilized to denigrate the lamas and their "superstitious practices," were also used to propagate "land reform." In the past the Tibetans, encouraged by their lamas, had refused to accept collectivization. Now they had no alternative, for anyone who dared to oppose the "reforms" was instantly branded as a counterrevolutionary and a criminal. As in the border areas, not only are the landless Tibetan herdsmen urged to denounce the "reactionary" herd owners but the poorer lamas also are encouraged to retail their sufferings at the hands of the richer lamas or Incarnate Lamas.

Heading this campaign is the Panchen Lama, who since being invested with political authority by the Chinese Communists has spearheaded the attack on the monasteries and obliquely even on some Buddhist practices. Thus in July His Serenity was quoted by Peking Radio as saying: "Things keep changing and developing. Some irrational religious systems should be constantly reformed. Temples and monasteries will inevitably be involved in the reforms since the temples and monasteries and some of the high-ranking lamas in them also possess manorial estates and are serf owners. It will not be beneficial to religion if the serfs of the aristocratic feudal government are emancipated while the serfs of the lamasaries remain in bondage." Such statements are inevitably accompanied by assurances that there will be no interference with the people's freedom of worship.

Peking's land reforms are pervasive and cover wide spheres of activity, for though ostensibly economic their purpose is political. The blow at the lamaist monasteries is calculated to eliminate the power of the Buddhist priesthood, whose estates are now in the process of being broken up. On the surface many of the reforms instituted by the Communists seem reasonable and accord with a widely quoted Han saying in Tibet: *Man man ti lai* (Slowly, but it will come). It certainly will; for as experience in China and the national minority areas proves, this tactic merely represents the thin end of the wedge which in time will prise wide open the entire political, economic, and social systems.

It is worth recalling in the light of what is happening in Tibet today what was promised to that country by the Chinese as late as April, 1956. At the inaugural meeting of the Preparatory Committee, General Chang Kuo-hua outlined what he described as "the established policy of the Central People's Government on the question of reforms in Tibet." According to him the Tibetan region differed greatly, socially and economically, from the areas of the Han people and the other minority nationalities. "The measures to be taken in future to carry out reforms in the Tibetan region must also be different from those adopted in other areas," the general assured his Tibetan audience. "Future reforms in the Tibet region must be carried out from the upper to the lower levels and by peaceful consultation, in accordance with the will and desire of the majority of the Tibetan people. During and after reforms, the government must take whatever steps are necessary to ensure that the political status and living conditions of the upper-class Tibetan people (including upper-class ecclesiastics) will not be reduced but will possibly be raised. That is to say: changes can only be for the better and not for the worse. This method is to the advantage of the aristocracy and of the monasteries and also of the people. After future reforms in Tibet the religious beliefs of the people can remain completely unchanged."

The brazen brashness and effrontery of these assurances in the context of later events reveal the cynicism underlying Communist promises. They were in fact endorsed at the same meeting by Chinese Vice Premier Chen Yi, who said: "The Communist party of China and the Central People's Government hold that reforms in Tibet can only be carried out when the Tibetan leaders and people unanimously demand them and are determined on them. They can never be carried out by any other nationality."

Today the Chinese in Tibet are engaged in "reforms" which, far from ensuring that the political status and living conditions of the upper-class Tibetan people—lay and secular—are not merely maintained but improved, are calculated to destroy both. No genuine democrat denies the need for changes in Tibet's political, economic, and social structure, and the Dalai Lama himself has expressed this view both before and after leaving Tibet. But what is taking place in that hapless country today represents the first step on the road to Communism which will end only with the "conversion" of Tibet into a Communist land absorbed in the great motherland of Han imperialism. Many of the reforms so far initiated by the Chinese Communists in Tibet would have been acceptable to the Dalai Lama and his government if their purpose had not been the consolidation of Han overlordship. Furthermore it was obvious that the Chinese were out to destroy traditional Tibetan values and to replace them by a superimposed Marxist ideology and rule.

Two-thirds of Tibet's population comprise agricultural and pastoral serfs living in a feudal economy which denies them wages, payment being made in the form of grain, crops, and other commodities which they help to produce. The vast majority of them are metaphorically chained to the land, and they cannot leave it without obtaining their landlord's permission and paying him compensation. The former is generally refused, while the latter is too often beyond the serf's resources. The Communist plan to abolish the system of unpaid, forced labor and to give the serfs freedom of their persons is therefore in principle unexceptionable. The Communists also plan to "buy out" landed estates from the manorial lords and redistribute them among the peasants, a measure whose justice will obviously depend on the amount of compensation which the Reds pay to the landlords. If past experience is any guide, this is nothing but a form of virtual expropriation. Lands belonging to the monasteries will also be "bought out," and the lamas are promised subsidies if the revenue from the land left to them is insufficient to support them. Debts owed up to the end of 1958 by the "laboring people" to the manorial lords are annulled. Freedom of worship is promised, but since the survival of each monastery depends on the loyalty of its inmates to the regime this constitutes a form of political blackmail holding up the lamas to ransom. Their ultimate fate is not likely to be vastly different from that of the erstwhile Buddhist monks and nuns in China who have been "persuaded" to leave their monasteries, engage in "productive labor," and marry. The Communist policy on the Tibetan religion, and its use as a political instrument, were foreshadowed in October, 1957, when General Chang Kuo-hua commented on the role he expected the Tibet branch of the China Buddhist Association to play. As reported in the Tibet *Jih Pao* of October 18th, Chang said: "In order to implement better the policy of religious freedom, it is the duty of the Tibetan Buddhist Association to transmit regularly and propagate to the Buddhists the policies, laws, and decrees of the Party and government; organize them to engage in study and positively take part in the anti-imperialist and patriotic campaign and the campaign for defending world peace, as well as in various constructive undertakings."

In short the Tibetan lamas, like the Panchen Lama, are expected to be the mouthpieces of their political masters.

india, china, and tibet

CHAPTER FIVE

In the period of British rule India's policy on Tibet was governed by the primary consideration of securing a buffer state between India and China from which Russia, at first tsarist and later Communist, would also be excluded. This was the underlying purpose of the successive conventions of Lhasa, Peking, St. Petersburg, and Simla.

Two years after India attained independence China became Communist, and the situation between India, China, and Tibet altered radically. It was Nehru's mistake that he continued to treat the situation as static on the specious plea that independent India's policy on Tibet was a heritage from the British raj. Lord Curzon, who was Viceroy of India at the time of the Younghusband expedition, had described Chinese suzerainty over Tibet as "a political affectation" and "a constitutional fiction" and had pressed for an "altered policy" to fill the vacuum which, he feared, Russia might occupy. Nehru's policy, it would seem, was activated principally by a desire to appease China while respecting Tibetan autonomy. Thereby he hoped to ensure his main aim, which was the preservation of the security and integrity of India.

In doing this he underestimated the strength of Han expansionism reinforced by the even more purposeful aggressiveness of Communist imperialism. It cannot be claimed that he was not forewarned. What the Russians did in Hungary, Czechoslovakia, Rumania, Poland, Bulgaria, and Albania the Chinese did in Tibet. In fact in 1959 the Chinese merely completed that which they had begun in 1950 and against which India, then as later, had protested ineffectually.

No reasonable person or government expected India to go to war with China over Tibet in 1950 or in 1959. But by refraining from recognizing Tibet as a sovereign, independent state between 1947 and 1949, at a time when neither the Chinese Communists nor the Nationalists could have effectively intervened, India lost the opportunity of bringing Tibet into the forum of independent nations and simultaneously of ensuring the existence of a buffer state between herself and China. That mistake might still cost India dearly. But its consequences were aggravated by New Delhi's attitude to China and Tibet in 1950, and again in 1959.

In both instances India began by protesting vigorously, but when faced with a *fait accompli* she meekly acquiesced. Had New Delhi supported the request of the El Salvador delegate in November, 1950, that the Tibetan plea should be heard by the United Nations it is possible that both the United States and Britain would have voted in its favor. The record of the U.N. proceedings suggests this. But the Indian attitude, as we shall see, was unfortunately equivocal. Similarly in 1959, having allowed the Dalai Lama and some 12,000 Tibetans asylum in India, the Government of India

appeared to be currying favor with the Chinese by announcing that it would again sponsor Communist China's admission to the U.N. Peking's reaction to New Delhi's humble
gesture has been one of lordly and calculated disdain, and
the U.N., as expected, has rejected the plea after a remarkably brief speech by the normally loquacious Krishna Menon.

The Chinese invasion of Tibet in October, 1950, while the
Tibetan mission was on its way from India to Peking, provoked a sharp exchange of communications between the Indian and Chinese governments. In its first note of October
26th the Indian Government complained that, despite the
fact that "we have been repeatedly assured of a desire by
the Chinese Government to settle the Tibetan problem by
peaceful means and negotiations," and notwithstanding the
departure of the Tibetan delegation for Peking on October
25th, the Chinese Government had ordered its troops to invade Tibet. Actually the invasion had already taken place
on October 7th, but Peking did not announce its decision
to move its troops until about October 25th. On October
30th the Chinese replied in pointedly sharp tones. "Tibet,"
Peking affirmed, "is an integral part of Chinese territory.
The problem of Tibet is entirely a domestic problem of
China. The Chinese People's Liberation Army must enter
Tibet, liberate the Tibetan people, and defend the frontiers of China. This is the resolved policy of the Central People's Government. . . . No foreign interference will be tolerated." The reference to defending the frontiers of China
in relation to Tibet is interesting, for the Tibetan frontiers
abut on India, Nepal, Bhutan, Sikkim, and Ladakh, the other
frontiers on the north and east abutting on China itself.
Peking's note went on to characterize the Indian viewpoint
as "deplorable" and as "having been affected by foreign influences hostile to China in Tibet."

In its second note, dated October 31st, New Delhi repudiated the Chinese charge that it was affected by foreign influences. Earlier, on October 8th, the U.N. forces in Korea had crossed the 38th parallel, and the Indian Government was anxious to contain the area of conflict. It accordingly appealed to the Chinese to refrain from doing anything "calculated to increase the present deplorable tensions of the world," emphasizing simultaneously that "Tibetan autonomy is a fact which, judging from reports they have received from other sources, the Chinese Government were themselves willing to recognize and foster." While reiterating that New Delhi had "no political or territorial ambitions" in Tibet, the Indian Government emphatically stated that "there was no justification whatever for such military operations" which represented "an attempt to impose a decision by force." On November 16th the Chinese Government replied, insisting that Tibet was an integral part of Chinese territory and that the problem of Tibet was entirely a domestic problem of China. Peking's note of November 16th makes some disquieting disclosures which New Delhi has so far not challenged. The note refers to an *aide-mémoire* dated August 28, 1950, by the Indian Government to the Chinese Government wherein, according to the latter, New Delhi had accepted Peking's view that "the regional autonomy granted by the Chinese Government to national minorities inside the country is an autonomy within the confines of Chinese sovereignty." The note also asserts that "on August 31 the Chinese Ministry of Foreign Affairs informed the Indian Government through Ambassador Panikkar that the Chinese People's Liberation Army was going to take action soon in west Sikang." New Delhi did not deny this, which suggests that at least a month before the Chinese actually launched their offensive on Tibet, New Delhi was aware of Peking's plan.

Looking back on these episodes, the Chinese strategy vis-à-vis India on Tibet emerges more clearly. Once Peking had decided on "liberating" Tibet, it was anxious to secure New Delhi's support or, at the very least, the Indian Government's noninterference. Seen in that light its actions assume a consistent pattern. First, Peking skillfully extracted an acknowledgment by New Delhi in the *aide-mémoire* referred to above that the Government of India recognized Chinese sovereignty over regionally autonomous Tibet. Having secured this, Peking next proceeded to inform New Delhi of its decision to act soon, thus attempting to make India privy to the Chinese plan. What the Indian Government's reactions to this were has not been disclosed, but consistent with its later attitude New Delhi probably urged China to settle the matter "peacefully." When China ignored this advice, all that India could do was to protest.

It could in fact have done more. On December 6th Nehru, speaking in the Lok Sabha, declared that India wanted the Sino-Tibetan question settled peacefully, and in a reference to Chinese talk of "liberating" Tibet confessed it was not clear to him from whom the Chinese were going to "liberate" Tibet. Yet when the helpless Tibetans turned to New Delhi, pleading with India to sponsor their case before the U.N., Lhasa was advised to appeal to the U.N. directly. This, in view of Tibet's ambiguous international status, could not be done by her except through a sponsor. Even so, the Tibetans assumed that India, having given this advice, would support their plea to the point of censuring China for using force against a helpless people. In this also they were doomed to disappointment. As Jayaprakash Narayan, well known once as a Socialist leader but now associated with Vinoba Bhave's Bhoodan (land renunciation) movement, observed: "It is true that we could not have prevented the Chinese from annexing Tibet. But we could have saved ourselves from being party to a wrong."

Unfortunately, India's attitude when the Tibetan appeal came up before the U.N. in November, 1950, was equivocal and, in the context of the facts, inexcusable. The representative of El Salvador in sponsoring Tibet's case pointed out that while Tibet was not a member of the U.N., a duty rested on that organization to maintain peace not only between member states but throughout the world. He urged the General Assembly not to dismiss the Tibetan case unheard. The Indian representative, the Jam Saheb of Nawanagar, in reply observed that India as a neighbor of China and Tibet, "with both of which it had friendly relations," was particularly anxious that the matter should be settled peacefully. The Chinese forces, he pointed out, had ceased to advance after the fall of Chamdo, "a town of some 480 kilometers from Lhasa." The Indian Government was certain that the Tibetan question could still be settled by peaceful means and that such a settlement could safeguard the autonomy which Tibet had enjoyed for several decades while maintaining its historical association with China.

By a coincidence which did not go unnoticed, the British representative, Mr. Younger, had earlier spoken in broadly the same terms as the Jam Saheb, and had proposed that the committee * should defer decision on the request made by the El Salvador delegate. The Jam Saheb concluded his speech by endorsing the British representative's suggestion. "My delegation," he observed, "consider that the best way of obtaining this objective [a peaceful settlement] is to abandon, for the time being, the idea of including this question in the agenda of the General Assembly." The Australian representative, Sir Keith Officer, dutifully concurred. That the United States only reluctantly agreed to this proposal was made clear by its representative, Mr. Ernest A. Gross. He had voted for adjournment, he explained, in view of the fact that the Gov-

* The General Committee of the U.N. General Assembly.

ernment of India, whose territory bordered on Tibet and which was therefore an interested party, had told the General Committee that it hoped that the Tibetan question would be peacefully and honorably settled. In accordance with its traditional policy, the United States would in usual circumstances have voted for the inclusion of the item in the General Assembly agenda. His government had always supported any proposal to refer to the U.N. international disputes or complaints of aggression, which could thus be aired, considered, and settled at international hearings. That was the principle applied by the United States Government even in the case of accusations made against the United States and despite the illogical and fraudulent nature of those accusations. However, in the present case, the United States delegation wanted to support the proposal made by the member states most directly concerned in the subject matter of the request submitted by the El Salvador delegation.

Like Czechoslovakia twelve years before, Tibet was sold down the river. The irony lay in Nehru's contrasting attitudes to these two tragedies. In 1938 he had visited Czechoslovakia while in Europe and had watched with growing irritation and dismay the devious strategy of Lord Runciman, who was endeavoring simultaneously to soften up the Nazi Henlein and, as Nehru put it, "to break the back of the Czechs." He had listened to the League of Nations as it debated on Czechoslovakia and was contemptuous of the entire proceedings. Did these thoughts recur to him when the Indian delegate, on New Delhi's instructions, assumed the same equivocal posture in the United Nations debate on Tibet?

An eastern Munich was not far away, and to that also India unhappily lent her imprimatur. Pledges and promises meaning nothing to the Communists, Peking signed an agreement with Tibet on May 23, 1951, recognizing Tibet's regional autonomy under the unified leadership of the Central People's

Government of China. We have seen how these pledges, easily given, were easily broken.

In 1950 Nehru, lulled by Communist China's assurances of her intention to reach a peaceful settlement with Tibet, not only induced that country to negotiate directly with Peking but persuaded the democratic nations of the U.N. to refrain from censuring China. The Communist armies, well aware of India's proclivities on this issue, had temporarily halted at Chamdo. They were marking time. No sooner did the U.N., on India's assurance, flash the green light than the Communists resumed their march on Lhasa. The Sino-Tibetan agreement, dictated by Peking and assuring Tibet of regional autonomy, was hailed as a great diplomatic victory in New Delhi and as an endorsement of the Government of India's farsighted policy. Events were to prove how nearsighted that policy was.

Charmed and beguiled by the "sweet reasonableness" of the Chinese, New Delhi went a step further. The British had recognized Chinese suzerainty over Tibet in return for Chinese recognition of Tibetan autonomy. India for no discernible reason proceeded beyond this. In the Sino-Indian treaty on Tibet of April, 1954, to which, incidentally, Tibet was not a signatory, India by implication recognized Chinese sovereignty as distinct from suzerainty. By dealing directly with China and ignoring Tibet, India officially recognized the special status of the former vis-à-vis the latter. Moreover, in the agreement itself it adopted the Chinese phrase, "the Tibet region of China," thereby impliedly recognizing Chinese sovereignty over Tibet. This interpretation is borne out by Nehru's speech in the Lok Sabha where the agreement was attacked by several members, including the veteran Congressman Purushottamdas Tandon, the late Dr. S. P. Mookerjee, Dr. Satya Narayan Sinha, and Dr. H. N. Kunzru. "Some criticism has been made that this is a recognition of Chinese sovereignty over Tibet," said the prime minister. "I am not aware of any time during the last few hundred years *when Chinese sovereignty or, if you like, suzerainty,* was challenged by any outside country, and all during this period whether China was weak or strong and, whatever the Government of China was, China always maintained this claim to sovereignty over Tibet." Clearly in Nehru's mind the distinction between suzerainty and sovereignty was of no great consequence. That was also the Chinese view.

The agreement, signed at Peking, dealt with trade and other matters concerning pilgrims between India and Tibet, and was to remain in force for eight years. It permitted Indian trade agencies to function in the Tibetan border towns of Yatung, Gyantse, and Gartok in return for Chinese trade agencies operating in India's capital, New Delhi, Kalimpong, and the leading commercial city of Calcutta. Certain markets for trade were specified in both countries. Traders and pilgrims, except "inhabitants of the border districts of the two countries who cross the borders to carry on petty trade or to visit friends and relatives," were required to hold entry certificates or permits in addition to the usual passports and visas. The agreement was confirmed in a subsequent note addressed by the Government of India to the Chinese Government wherein New Delhi undertook to withdraw within six months the military escort which had been stationed at Yatung and Gyantse ever since the Lhasa Convention of 1904 for the protection of Indian pilgrims and traders. It also promised to hand over to the Government of China, "at a reasonable price," the post, telegraph, and public telephone services together with their equipment operated by the Government of India in "the Tibet region of China." New Delhi later decided, "as a gesture of good will," to waive its claim to compensation for the postal, telegraph, and telephone equipment in Tibet.

The preamble to the Sino-Indian agreement on Tibet enunciated for the first time the now famous five principles of coexistence known in India as *Panchshila,** which though not formally accepted by all the countries of Asia and Africa, notably Pakistan, Thailand, South Viet Nam, Malaya, Tunis, and Morocco, is still regarded by them as an intangible safeguard against the incursions of Red China. The preamble reads: "The Government of the Republic of India and the Central People's Government of the People's Republic of China, being desirous of promoting trade and cultural intercourse between the Tibet region of China and India and of facilitating pilgrimage and travel by the peoples of China and India, have resolved to enter into the present agreement based on the following principles: (1) Mutual respect for territorial integrity and sovereignty (2) Nonaggression (3) Noninterference in internal affairs (4) Equality and mutual benefit (5) Peaceful coexistence."

The principles of Panchshila were reiterated and reaffirmed in a joint statement by the prime ministers of India and China in June, 1954, when Chou En-lai visited New Delhi, and in April, 1955, the principles were incorporated in the final communiqué of the Afro-Asian Conference at Bandung in Indonesia. If pious verbal assurances of this character really meant what they said, the world would by now have talked itself into peace. Nehru's misguided trust lay in accepting without question Chinese assurances of good faith and good conduct, although the experience of Tibet in 1950, which exposed simultaneously the character of Han expansionism and Communist imperialism, should have warned him against any such facile belief.

At Bandung, Chou En-lai was to wear the same mask and deceive not only India but many countries of Asia and Africa. Never was the calculated cynicism and opportunism of Com-

* The word means "five tenets."

munist China more skillfully deployed than at this Afro-Asian conference where Chou blandly assured the small nations of Asia that they had nothing to fear from their big neighbor China, even though at that very time Peking was in the process of "softening up" Tibet for the final kill. Where the borderline between China and a neighboring country had not yet been fixed, announced Chou, his country was willing to do so "by peaceful means." China had demonstrated in Tibet and Korea what she understood by that phrase. Doubtless in good time the same means would be employed to settle the frontier between China on the one hand and India and Burma on the other.

In the Lok Sabha, shortly after the signing of the Sino-Indian agreement, Nehru, faced with criticism that the Indian Government had shown great weakness in dealing with the Chinese on Tibet, particularly in admitting that China had full authority over Tibet or that China was controlling Tibet, defended the agreement firmly. "In my opinion," he asserted, "we have done no better thing than this since we became independent. I have no doubt about this. . . . I think it is right for our country, for Asia and for the world." The critics had fastened on the withdrawal of the Indian military escorts from Yatung and Gyantse. "Is it proper that troops of our country should be stationed in another independent country?" the prime minister demanded. "The number of troops was not too large, barely three hundred, but what does it indicate? What right does India have to keep a part of her army in Tibet, whether Tibet is independent or a part of China? The British Empire in the days of Lord Curzon, about fifty years ago, had expanded into and made several types of arrangements in Tibet. Now it is impossible and improper for us to continue any such arrangements as the British Empire had established." If so, the question naturally arose: Why then accept the British "imperialist" concept of

Chinese suzerainty over Tibet? Either India accepted the British legacy wholesale or not at all. To pick and choose was to be selective at the cost of China or Tibet, and to expose oneself to the charge of being guided more by expediency than by principle.

Dr. Satya Narayan Sinha, in criticizing the Indian Government's attitude to Tibet, had referred to various treaties and maps going back to the period of British rule in India. According to Dr. Sinha these documents proved that independent India had gone further than the British had done in their commitments to China. Nehru contemptuously brushed aside these charges. "Let me tell him," he declared answering Dr. Sinha, "these treaties and maps were all prepared by British imperialists. These treaties and maps are intended to show that we must act as they did." In saying this, the prime minister overlooked one fact: that he himself had accepted Chinese suzerainty over Tibet as a political legacy from the British. He also did not anticipate that the Communist Chinese themselves would so adjust their maps that they would ultimately prepare a blueprint for a Himalayan federation consisting of Nepal, Sikkim, Bhutan, Ladakh, and parts of India's Northeast Frontier Agency, to function doubtless under Chinese sovereignty or, in the prime minister's words, "if you like, suzerainty."

The integrity and security of India must inevitably govern that foreign policy which, like that of every country, is motivated by "enlightened self-interest." India's prime minister was obviously impressed by the Communist revolution in China which repeated after the Second World War what the Bolsheviks had succeeded in establishing in Russia in the closing years of the First. "Now we must realize," Nehru apostrophized his audience in the Lok Sabha, "that this revolution that came to China is the biggest thing that has taken place in the world at present, whether you like it or not.

. . . For the first time in several hundred years of history China now has a strong central government. This fact is a very important fact for Asia and the world." Those who do not know Nehru would immediately accuse him of thereby placing might before right. Nothing could have been further from his mind; but from the language he used even the Communist Chinese can be excused for reading into it the conclusion which the Indian prime minister's critics deduced.

In the same speech Nehru referred to Panchshila in words which the hindsight of history exposes as both pathetic and prophetic. "Live and let live," he proclaimed. "No one should invade the other, no one should fight the other. . . . This is the basic principle which we have put in our treaty with China."

In the light of China's ruthless aggression on Tibet in 1959, the assurances are ironic. "These," said India's prime minister, referring to Panchshila, "are words we have used: 'recognition of territorial integrity and sovereignty, nonaggression, noninterference,' and we consider other things like 'mutuality.' Now 'territorial integrity' and 'sovereignty' mean that there should be no invasion. 'Nonaggression' also means the same thing, and 'noninterference' means that there should be no interference in domestic affairs because some people are in the habit of interfering in other people's affairs."

The puzzle is why Nehru, confronted with accumulating evidence of Chinese duplicity and bad faith, should have continued to take Peking's promises on trust. Surely he had read his Marx and Lenin and remembered Lenin's dictum that "in the battle for the victory of socialism every means is allowed." Did India's prime minister believe that Peking was making a distinction between the West and Asia and was bound to the latter by fraternity and blood? Or did he feel that the Communists used the methods of duplicity and force only against the capitalist world? Russia had pledged to respect the freedom of the peoples of East Europe in the Yalta Agreement, and thereafter had proceeded to subjugate Czechoslovakia, Rumania, Hungary, Poland, Bulgaria, and Albania, all of which had desired to be friendly with her. In the Communist code friendliness is not enough, and international agreements are respected only so long as they are advantageous. China was shortly to give a proof of peaceful coexistence in Tibet.

In 1956 the Dalai Lama and the Panchen Lama visited India, and also in India at the time was the Chinese prime minister. The Dalai Lama has since revealed * that he was even at that time acutely unhappy over the situation in Tibet. "As I was unable to do anything for the benefit of my people," he confessed, "I had practically made up my mind when I came to India not to return to Tibet until there was a manifest change in the attitude of the Chinese authorities." In this predicament the Dalai Lama sought the advice of the Indian prime minister, who, as His Holiness acknowledged, "has always shown me unfailing kindness and consideration." Nehru thereupon spoke to Chou En-lai, who promptly gave him the usual assurances, which as usual Nehru accepted at their face value. He assured the Dalai Lama that all would be well, and urged him to return to his country. "I followed his advice," said His Holiness, "and returned to Tibet in the hope that conditions would change substantially for the better. And I have no doubts that my hopes would have been realized if the Chinese authorities had on their part carried out the assurances which the Chinese prime minister had given to the prime minister of India. It was, however, painfully clear soon after my return that the representatives of the Chinese Government had no intention of adhering to their promises. The natural and inevita-

* In his statement of June 20, 1959.

ble result was that the situation daily grew worse until it became impossible to control the spontaneous upsurge of my people against the tyranny and oppression of the Chinese authorities."

What were the assurances which Chou En-lai so glibly gave and which Nehru so easily accepted? A clue was given by the Indian prime minister in a speech in the Lok Sabha on March 30, 1959. "When Mr. Chou En-lai was last in India," said Nehru, "he laid stress first of all that Tibet was and had always been a part of the Chinese State, part of the larger family of China. Then he said that Tibet was not a province of China. It was different from China proper, and he recognized that and therefore we [India] consider it an autonomous region of the Chinese State. The Chinese people are called the Han people. The Tibetans are not Hans. Tibetans are Tibetans."

Chou, however, clearly did not mean what he said. In Nehru's view China, while claiming Tibet as part of its larger family, recognized Tibet's regional autonomy, and had no desire to assimilate it by making it a province or part and parcel of China. This, however, is precisely Communist China's aim, for the Chinese Constitution, unlike the Soviet Constitution, does not give the national minorities the right of secession. The Communist Chinese aim has always been to assimilate the national minorities, including the Tibetans, and to absorb them totally within the political, economic, and social structure of the Communist State. According to the Chinese the Tibetan view is irrelevant in the overriding context of the Chinese concept of the state.

This is contrary to the orthodox Marxist-Leninist approach to nationality, though it is not the only instance where Mao Tse-tung has deviated from the recognized line. When the Bolsheviks seized power in Russia under Lenin, they proclaimed the right of self-determination, including the right of secession as a fundamental right of the national minorities, though in practice no nationality has been allowed to exercise that right. Article 15 of the Soviet Constitution states, "The U.S.S.R. protects the sovereign rights of the Union Republics," while Article 17 says, "The right freely to secede from the U.S.S.R. is reserved to every Union Republic." The fact that the right is theoretical undoubtedly detracts from the principle, but it is of interest in so far as it shows that the Communist Chinese attitude to the national minorities is both theoretically and in practice more rigid than that of the Soviet.

Initially the Communist Chinese approach was similar to that of the Soviet Union. In the 1931 Constitution of the so-called Kiangsi Soviet of which Mao Tse-tung was chairman, the national minorities were promised the right of self-determination and secession from any Union of Chinese Soviets that might be established in the future. In his statement "On Coalition Government," published in 1945, Mao reaffirmed this by suggesting that the various races should form a Union of Democratic Republics of China. In 1949, however, when the Communist Chinese State was founded, the idea of independent republics was dropped in favor of "autonomous areas," and the Common Program by which the new government was guided made no mention of the right of secession. The National Constitution of Communist China, which was promulgated in 1954, went further. It stated unequivocally that China is "a unified, multinational State."

Federalism is an idea foreign to the Chinese, who regard themselves more as a civilization than as a nation, and a civilization in which anyone can be accepted. Hence the inherent expansionist thrust in Chinese society and civilization which makes it far more propulsive than that of the U.S.S.R.

The Indian Communist party's attitude to national minorities inclines toward Soviet policy but goes further. Not only does it support the right of self-determination, including the right of secession for linguistic minorities, but in the 1940's it actively promoted the creation of Pakistan by backing up the Moslem League's claim to a separate Islamic State. As long as it functions within a democratic state, this will probably be the policy of the Indian Communist party, but in the unhappy event of Communism coming to India it is likely that the Red attitude to the linguistic minorities will approximate to that of Communist China. Despite their present policy in India, the Indian Communists were vociferous in their support of Peking's action in Tibet, forgetting for the moment their own proclaimed adherence to national self-determination.

Nehru's adherence to peaceful coexistence automatically implies tolerance for a Communist party functioning in India. Indeed, the Indian President, Dr. Rajendra Prasad, once described Kerala, then under Communist rule, as a beautiful example of coexistence. But the Indian Communist party is the Trojan horse of international Communism in India. When criticism of Communist China mounted shortly after the Dalai Lama's flight from Lhasa and tempers ran high, the Chinese Embassy in Delhi summoned some Indian Reds for a briefing. As a result these Peking patriots dutifully echoed their master's voice and were not ashamed to say so. "The People's Government of China, in all sincerity, has asked us to look into this matter," a Communist leader confessed in the Lok Sabha. As we have noted earlier, the National Council of the Indian Communist party passed a resolution supporting China's action in Tibet, and its spokesmen in Parliament upheld Peking's charge that the Tibetan revolt was Indian-inspired and that Kalimpong was the command center of a revolt by "feudal elements" in Tibet against the "people." The reaction of other parties to the Communist attitude was indignant, some members demanding that

India's chief election commissioner should cancel the Communist party's accreditation as a national party. "The Communists," commented Nehru, "cease to be Indians, having shown a total absence of feelings of decency and nationality."

If the general Indian reaction to China's aggression on Tibet was sharp and angry, the Government of India initially pursued a more cautious and less consistent course. When early in March, 1959, the Indian prime minister was questioned in the Lok Sabha on reports reaching India of clashes between the Tibetans and Chinese, Nehru deprecated such accounts as colorful and exaggerated, and described the reported clash as "a conflict of minds." This phrase should rank high in any list of political euphemisms. When the Dalai Lama visited India in 1956 he extended an invitation to the Indian prime minister to visit Tibet, but when in the fall of 1958 Nehru proposed to go to Lhasa he was cryptically asked to postpone his visit. Even after the fact of the uprising in Lhasa was world news, New Delhi remained circumspect. The matter was again raised in Parliament late in March when the Chinese accused India of allowing Kalimpong to be used as "a commanding center of rebellion," a charge which Nehru had repudiated three days earlier. "This is a difficult and delicate situation," said the prime minister, "and we should avoid doing anything which will worsen it. We have no intention of interfering in the internal affairs of China, with whom we have friendly relations. In 1954 the Sino-Indian agreement was concluded. It was in this that for the first time the principle of Panchshila was stated. . . . India wishes to have friendly relations with the people of Tibet and wants them to progress in freedom. At the same time it is important for us to have friendly relations with that great country China. That does not mean that I, the Government or the Indian Parliament or anyone else should submit to any kind of dictation from any country, howsoever great it may be. But it does mean that in a difficult situation we should exercise a certain measure of restraint and wisdom in dealing with the situation and not in excitement do something which will lead our country into difficulties."

Wise words, and in the context justifiable. But their wisdom and justification depended on how they would be implemented. New Delhi's official attitude was politically impeccable, but newspaper correspondents at this time were interested to notice that in some official circles another line was privately canvassed. Nehru had expressed India's wish to see Tibet "progress in freedom," and it was subtly implied that the Chinese were helping this progress by undermining Tibet's feudal society. It was a line sedulously peddled by the Communists and fellow travelers, as well as by their sympathizers inside and outside the citadel of the government. Jayaprakash Narayan made the most effective retort to these transparent tactics. "It is said," he remarked, "that even if the Chinese are behaving a little roughly in Tibet, why be so squeamish about it? Are they not forcibly rescuing the Tibetan masses from medieval backwardness and forcing them toward progress and civilization? It is strange that as soon as some people put themselves outside their own country, they become screaming imperialists. If the right is conceded to nations to thrust progress forcibly down the throats of other nations, why were the British not welcomed as torchbearers of progress in India?" The issue also depended, as Jayaprakash Narayan went on to say, on what one meant by human progress. Did one equate it with industrialization, rising production statistics, communes, and sputniks? He preferred another view that saw progress in terms of humanity —the growth of human freedom, the decline of selfishness and cruelty, the spread of tolerance and cooperation.

If Nehru thought that his verbal rebukes would halt the Chinese in their aggressive tactics and induce a reexamination of conscience, he was mistaken. No sooner did the Chinese realize that the Dalai Lama was heading for India than they loosed a vituperative barrage against India which later they were to reinforce by troop movements along the Indo-Tibetan border. The New China News Agency spearheaded this attack with a series of reports and comments accusing Indians of "expansionist aims" in Tibet, and this theme provided the keynote for the subsequent stream of virulent abuse directed against India. "Some Indian papers," lamented the NCNA, "openly advocated to convene a conference by India to discuss the rebellion in Tibet which was purely China's internal affair. Such an absurd advocation fully reflected the conspiracy and ambition of the Indian expansionists." In Bombay followers of the Indian Praja Socialist party and other groups had demonstrated before the Chinese Consulate, hurling rotten tomatoes at posters of Mao Tse-tung and shouting slogans such as "Long Live Free Tibet!" "Down with Stalinists!" and so on. In an angry tirade the NCNA denounced these "slanderous slogans against China," referred to the "ravings" of Indian politicians over the "rebellion in Tibet" and harped again on "Indian expansionism." Even the pro-Communist Bombay weekly *Blitz,* which, following the Red line, had justified Peking's aggression on Tibet, was taken to task by the NCNA for making "a nonsensical suggestion." This was a proposal for a tripartite conference of India, China, and Tibet. The NCNA, while commending *Blitz's* general attitude, complained: "The editor of the weekly in this open letter completely disregarded the fact that Tibet is an integral part of China and that the rebellion in Tibet is China's internal affair which allows no foreign intervention." More specifically the Chinese attacked the views expressed by the Congress party president, Mrs. Indira Gandhi, daughter of Nehru, who had sponsored a Citizens' Committee in Delhi to organize relief for the Tibetan refugees. Their ire was aroused by a speech wherein Mrs. Gandhi, according to the NCNA, "attempted to defend the stand of India on the Tibet question." All that Mrs. Gandhi had said was that "India's stand on the Tibetan issue and the granting of asylum to the Dalai Lama were in keeping with the country's tradition and its independent foreign policy."

Peking objected violently to "the conspicuous notice" which the Dalai Lama was receiving in India and to the "unusual reception" accorded him. Here it scented a device to condemn China indirectly, and in proof quoted an article by Prem Bhatia, the well-known editor of the *Tribune* of Ambala, Punjab. Bhatia had written: "The highly probable explanation of such a reception, and one which is much more important in terms of foreign policy, is Nehru's wish to express indirect disapproval of China's stand over Tibet. While India cannot with complete justification sermonize the Chinese over what has been accepted as the internal affair of China she can . . . make her attitude known through this oblique condemnation of China's bad faith."

Had New Delhi at this juncture maintained a firm and correct attitude, Indian repercussions to China's aggression on Tibet would have crystallized in a consistent mold. But Nehru preferred to be circumspect. Although an overwhelming proportion of the press and public opinion was deeply stirred against China, Nehru leaned backward to preserve the old cordial relations with Peking. The daily newspaper *National Herald* which he founded in the days before independence and in which he still takes intimate interest, declared editorially that "certain parties and individuals in this country [India] have no doubt been striving to utilize developments in Tibet to malign China and undermine Sino-Indian friendship." Nehru meanwhile continued to proclaim and protest India's friendship for China. Although he publicly rebuked the Chinese for using "the language of cold war," and repudiated their accusations and calumnies as "unbecoming and entirely void of substance," he reiterated constantly the need for Sino-Indian friendship. After visiting the Dalai Lama at Mussoorie in April, 1959, Nehru, talking to newspaper correspondents, expressed a desire to create conditions for the return of the Dalai Lama to Tibet, and urged that this as well as other matters "should not be the subject of heated exchanges and debates." They had to be considered quietly with a view to preventing the situation from getting worse.

The Chinese, however, were in no mood to reciprocate these soothing gestures. They stepped up their verbal barrage against India, reinforcing it with hostile acts. "The People's Republic of China," insisted a writer in the *People's Daily* of Peking, "enjoys full sovereignty over the Tibet region just as it does over the regions of Inner Mongolia, Sinkiang, Kwangsi, and Ninghsia. There can be no doubt whatever about this, and no interference by any foreign country or by the United Nations under whatever pretext or in whatever form will be tolerated." The more moderate New Delhi's tone became, the more aggressive grew Peking's attitude.

When on June 20th the Dalai Lama in an interview with newspaper correspondents declared, "Wherever I am, accompanied by my ministers, the Tibetan people recognize us as the Government of Tibet," New Delhi issued a statement ten days later that the Government of India did not recognize any separate Government of Tibet and that there was no question of a Tibetan Government under the Dalai Lama functioning in India. In reply the Dalai Lama a fortnight later stated that what he had said represented "a historical truth." His Holiness affirmed that the Panchen Lama had no *locus standi* and his government was "a deceptive one." In July the Government of India announced that it would again press at the next U.N. session for the admission of Communist China to the United Nations.

If New Delhi reckoned that by these gestures it would mollify Peking, the Communist Chinese soon disabused the Indian Government of the notion. Not only did the Red tirade continue but it was now accompanied by pointedly unfriendly acts to India. Indian and Nepalese traders were branded as "bloodsuckers," and Nehru, though not openly labeled a "running dog of imperialism," was impliedly accused of being in league with the so-called "upper strata" in Tibet, particularly the lamas who were denounced as "yellow brigands and red robbers." Every effort was made to discourage Tibetan traders from dealing with their counterparts in India, thereby making it difficult for the Indians, who were now suspect, to function normally in Tibet. Simultaneously through a hate campaign the Chinese attempted to stir up hostility to the Indians among the Tibetans as a counter to the latter's continuing loyalty to the Dalai Lama. While the anti-Indian campaign temporarily subsided after a while in China, it was continued in Tibet where it was virulently waged at certain trade centers like Gyantse. Later it was revived in China. Until 1955 a small Indian military force had been stationed in Gyantse, which still harbors memories of the Younghusband expedition, following which an Indian military force had been quartered at the town. Communist propaganda, carried on through bulletins and broadsheets and by word of mouth, described the Indians as inheritors of British imperialist traditions, with expansionist aims in Tibet. Indian nationals in that country were now subjected by the Chinese to various forms of harassment, primarily by interference with their trade. The majority of these traders come from Ladakh, and some of them have married Tibetan women. On the ground that a Tibetan woman though married to a foreigner retains her nationality, several Ladakhi traders were asked to quit Tibet, leaving their wives and families behind.

Indian officials were also subjected to petty harassments and humiliations. The Indian Trade Agent in western Tibet, Laxman Singh Jangepani, normally spends the summer months at various trade marts in his area, returning to India for the winter. In June, two months after the Dalai Lama was given asylum in India, Jangepani obtained a visa from the Chinese Embassy in New Delhi which specified that he should enter Tibet by the Niti Pass. This was convenient for him, as in returning to India during the previous October he had left his tents and other heavy equipment near the Tibetan end of the pass. After a journey of over three weeks Jangepani reached a Chinese checkpost in the Niti Pass and was coldly informed that he could not proceed by that route but should go by way of the Lepuleh Pass near the eastern border of Nepal and some three weeks' journey from the Niti Pass. This meant, apart from the personal discomfort and hardship involved, that the Indian trade agent would be able to spend only three months out of the four months' trading season in western Tibet.

Meanwhile the inflow of Tibetan refugees into India continued, and has now reached a total of nearly thirteen thousand, including some six thousand Khambas. Camps were initially set up for these refugees in Assam and West Bengal from where they are now being dispersed to various parts of the country, mostly to the mountainous northeast, and to Sikkim, where around three thousand refugees have settled and found work, mainly on road construction. It is possible that some of the Khambas will be settled in the Northeast Frontier Agency. The biggest resettlement problem is posed by the lamas, who number nearly three thousand, but efforts are being made in consultation with the Dalai Lama to place them in Buddhist monasteries in India, Bhutan, and Sikkim. To date, not a single one of the Tibetan refugees has asked to be sent back to his homeland. Among non-Indian agencies the Cooperative for American Relief Everywhere, Inc. (CARE), has played a most useful part. Food provided by CARE was waiting for the first refugees who reached the camps near Tezpur in Assam in mid-May, and the organization undertook to supply the basic ration for up to eight thousand people. Self-help programs were also devised to enable the refugees to learn new skills, apart from their traditional skills, such as wood and metalworking, bootmaking, the painting of Tibetan religious pictures, the weaving of Tibetan aprons and small rugs, the care of sheep and other livestock. Arrangements are also being made by CARE to find places for Tibetan scholars and students in universities, museums, and other institutions overseas so as to help them to go out into the world to study engineering mechanics, agriculture, medicine, and much else "to build a new Tibet."

The areas where these refugees are for the most part now being rehabilitated are regions which the Communist Chinese have cartographically already appropriated to themselves, despite India's protests. Chinese maps show many thousands of square miles of Indian territory spread over the Northeast Frontier Agency, along with Bhutan, Sikkim, Nepal, and Ladakh, as belonging to the People's Republic. At the same time Peking blandly assures New Delhi that "China never has interfered and never will interfere in India." In 1958 Nehru, speaking in the Lok Sabha, disclosed that Indian grazing lands on the Tibetan border had been forcibly occupied by Chinese herdsmen. Even before the Dalai Lama's flight to India a party of Indian officers, skiing in the Ladakh region of Kashmir, were suddenly kidnaped by some members of the Chinese Army on the ground that they had trespassed on territory belonging to the People's Republic. A similar incident occurred on the Indo-Tibetan border in the Indian state of Uttar Pradesh where ten Indian Army men were arrested by superior Chinese forces, taken across the border, interrogated, and then returned to the frontier blindfolded.

More recently the Communist Chinese have ceased even to pretend good will for India. Shortly after the Indian Government announced that it would again press for Communist China's admission into the U.N., Nehru disclosed in the Lok Sabha that the Chinese authorities had passed orders declaring Indian and Tibetan currencies illegal in Tibet. It was not clear, said India's prime minister, whether this order had been enforced. "However," he added, "it is not in keeping with the spirit of the 1954 Sino-Indian agreement."

Nehru also admitted that India's trade with Tibet had suffered very considerably "after the disturbances in Tibet." Indian imports from Tibet had dropped from Rs.15 lakhs ($300,000) in February, 1959, to Rs. 2 lakhs ($40,000) in June, 1959, exports during the same period dropping from Rs.10 lakhs ($200,000) to Rs. 3 lakhs ($60,000). Nehru confirmed that Indian traders in Lhasa were facing many difficulties: "Sometimes they could not travel about. Sometimes they could not get transport to carry their goods."

All this is part of a planned pattern. New Delhi has lodged more than one protest with Peking against these flagrantly discriminatory practices, but Peking has ostentatiously ignored the protests, and continues its calculated policy of harassment. Merchandise held by Indian traders has been frozen, and in some cases entire stocks have been "purchased" by the Chinese at arbitrary prices. Various payment difficulties have been artificially created. In certain areas stocks of Tibetan wool traditionally purchased by the Indians have been bought up by the Chinese. Although Nepal's trade with western Tibet has also suffered, owing partly to unsettled conditions, the Chinese have adopted a policy of treating the Nepalese better than the Indians, thereby planning to play off the one against the other. Pressure on Indian traders varies with localities. It is less strong in western and southern Tibet, traditionally supplied from India, than in the central and eastern regions. Local transborder trade has not yet been seriously affected, but obviously the Chinese plan to orientate the entire economy of Tibet toward China. External trade with India, as we noted, has slumped steeply, and the time is not far away when such external trade as Tibet is permitted will pass into the hands of monopoly official agencies.

All this constitutes a clear breach of the 1954 Sino-Indian Trade Agreement on Tibet whose preamble enshrined Panchshila. The agreement was made with the specific purpose "of promoting trade and cultural intercourse" between Tibet and India, and the fourth of the five tenets of Panchshila postulates "equality and mutual benefit." Neither exists today in Tibet.

the
world
outside

CHAPTER SIX

Tibet's history is very largely the history of a struggle to maintain her independence against foreign countries which schemed for political mastery. The most aggressive of these was China, but there were others, notably Britain, Russia and, in a much smaller degree, Nepal. Over the centuries the chief concern of the Tibetans has been twofold—to preserve their religion and to maintain their independence.

Although little is known historically of Tibet before the seventh century of the Christian era,* legend and tradition tell of links with China and India long before that time. While the Chinese association with Tibet even in this dim period was motivated very largely by expansionist aims, that of India has always been religious, cultural, and commercial. Even in the some two hundred years of British rule in India,

* The first source of this knowledge was Chinese. "The History of the Yuan Dynasty" (1280–1368) enumerates the administrative divisions of Tibet under the Mongol emperors, but there are earlier references to Tibet in Chinese historical documents.

144

interest in Tibet was primarily concerned with trade until late in the nineteenth century when the contending rivalries of Britain, China, and Russia made it political.

According to Tibetan folklore the very origin of the Tibetans, as we have seen, derives from the marriage of an ogress with a monkey identified as the Hindu deity Hanuman, a protégé of the Lord of Mercy who is called Avalokiteshwara by Indians and Chen-re-si by Tibetans.

The early legendary kings of Tibet commence with Nya-tri Tsen-po, who is said to have been the fifth son of the Indian King Prasenojit of Kosala. Today the Tibetan language, which consists of several dialects, is allied most intimately with the Burmese family of languages, but the link between the two is provided by the dialects spoken in the Himalayas and in North Assam. The Tibetan-Burman languages are closely related to Chinese and, less closely, to Thai, but it is a historical fact that during the reign of Song-tsan Gampo in the seventh century after Christ, the king sent scholars to India to fetch Buddhist scriptures and another to Kashmir to devise a Tibetan alphabet. This was done, the script being modeled on the Brahmi characters of Devanagari Sanskrit. A form of grammar was also introduced, and translations were made from Pali and Sanskrit manuscripts. Only in the fifteenth century, under the patronage of the Ming emperors, did Tibetan scholars turn to Chinese literature, which in time was to influence Tibetan ideas and writing. The Lamaist scriptures, compiled mostly between the eighth and thirteenth centuries, are for the major part translations from Sanskrit and Pali texts, though a few come from Chinese sources.

In other cultural fields, as in religion, Tibet has been affected greatly by India. Thus Tibetan art, particularly in the realm of painting, shows strong Indian influences going back to the medieval Buddhist art of Bihar and Orissa, which under the Pala kings were the strongholds of Indian Buddhism during the eleventh and twelfth centuries. Legend relates that the most ancient Buddhist sculpture imported into Tibet came from Magadha or South Bihar (a district intimately associated with the development of Buddhism) but that it reached Tibet by way of China, having been brought there by Wen Cheng, the Chinese princess who married King Song-tsan Gampo. This statue is preserved in the Jokhang temple in Lhasa. Both sculpture and painting in Tibet, like language, came in time under Chinese influences, so that Tibetan art might be said ultimately to have acquired three aspects—Indian, Chinese, and Tibetan. An interesting example of an Indian form is the swastika which the Tibetans paint on walls, pillars, and lintels on the eve of their New Year and which is reminiscent of the *rangoli* drawn on the floors of Indian households during the Hindu New Year.

Tibetan medical science has also borrowed heavily from the Indian Ayur-Veda, or indigenous system of herbal treatment, though wide recourse is made in case of illness to spells, incantations, and the exorcism of evil spirits. Again, the Tibetan calendar shows traces of Hindu astrology. Its cycle of sixty years is divided into five twelve-year groups based on the five elements which accord with the Indian *panch-mahabhoot*—earth, water, fire, iron, and wood.

In the domain of religion India's impact has been strongest. Buddhism came to Tibet early in the sixth century, but not until around A.D. 650 in the reign of Tsong-tsan Gampo was Buddhism established as a state religion. According to Tibetan tradition the first Buddhist objects are said to have fallen from heaven on the palace of King Lha-to To-ri Nyantsan, but in all likelihood they came from Nepal. After the advent of Buddhism in Tibet there was a flow of earnest scholars from that country to India, where students from other countries such as China, Cambodia, and Java also converged to study the *Tripitaka* and Buddhist tomes like the *Lalita-Vistara,* which is the chief source of the legend of the Buddha's life. The first Indian scholar to cross the Himalayas to the Roof of the World was the Tantric teacher Padma Sambhava who, as we have seen, founded Lamaism late in the eighth century and is revered as the patron saint of the Red Hat sect, followers of the Tantric form of Lamaist Buddhism. In 1013 the Indian pundit Dharmapala came to Tibet accompanied by his disciples, and he was followed early in the eleventh century by another Indian sage, Atisha, founder of the Red Hat sect which was to be reorganized some three centuries later by Tsong Ka-pa, the new form being known as the Yellow Hat sect. It is worth noting that Lamaism was first opposed by the Chinese Buddhists, one of whom named Hwa Shang protested against the teachings of Padma Sambhava, but he is said to have been defeated in argument and expelled from Tibet. The religious link between India and Tibet was strong enough, until the Communist advent, to see a yearly flow of Tibetan pilgrims to Bodh-Gaya in India where Gautama became the Buddha, and in the other direction of Hindus to Mount Kailasa in western Tibet where the deity Siva is supposed to reside with his consort Parvati. The Tibetans also regard Mount Kailasa, which they call Kang Rimpoche, as their holiest mountain; to both Hindus and Tibetans the Himalayan Mountains are sacred. Mount Kailasa overlooks Lake Mansarovar, again a place of pilgrimage for Hindus and Tibetans. In Hindu as well as in Buddhist cosmography Mount Kailasa is identified with Sumeru, the cosmic center of the earth, and Mansarovar is said by Hindus to have been created by the God Brahma's mental projection.

Trade between India and Tibet goes back almost to time immemorial. Tibetan exports consist largely of raw wool furs, hides and skins, rock salt, borax, medicinal herbs, and *pasham,* the soft underwool of the shawl goat. Ponies and mules are also exported, along with Tibetan metalwork and jewelry, more often than not heavily set with turquoises. The largest market of the Tibetan wool trade is Kalimpong, through which passes quite half the entire trade between India and Tibet. Indian exports include cotton goods, food grains, precious stones, corals, tobacco, hardware, and miscellaneous stores. From China before Communist days Tibet received silk, satin, brocade, cotton goods, and brick tea. It used to be said that the Chinese emperor exploited tea and silk to control Tibet.

In pre-Communist days most of the merchandise from the outside world was brought in by an almost continuous train of mule caravans, and the Lhasa Bazar made a colorful spectacle with traders from Sikkim, Bhutan, Nepal, Ladakh, and from Kalimpong and northern India. The caravan routes still operate, but the construction by the Chinese of two major highways linking Tibet closer with China, as well as the new network of internal roads capable of carrying traffic by motor trucks, might soon displace the muleteers on the old trails. Today the most important trade route between India and Tibet starts from Kalimpong in the district of Darjeeling, running through Gangtok, capital of Sikkim, through Nathu La * into the Chumbi Valley to Phari. There is another route, also starting from Kalimpong, which traverses Sikkim to enter Tibet by the Jelep La. From Phari, before the construction of the Sikang-Tibet highway, there were two routes to Lhasa—one skirting the eastern side of Hram Tso (Otter Lake) and the other through Gyantse, the latter being the longer route. With the extension of the Sikang-Tibet road southwest to Shigatse and through Gyantse to Phari, the Chinese have come up almost to the mouth of Nathu La. There are other passes leading from western Tibet into Sik-

* La means Pass.

kim and Bhutan, such as the Niti Pass and the Lepuleh Pass near the eastern border of Nepal.

China's relations with Tibet, unlike those of India, have never contented themselves with being cultural and commercial. With the Mongols, Mings, Manchus, the Kuomintang, and Communists, and even in prehistoric days, commerce and culture have served primarily as instruments of political domination.

From ancient times the vast majority of China's northern and northwestern neighbors were nomadic peoples like the Mongols and Tibetans. An old Chinese pictograph of a Tchiang, or Tibetan, shows a man driving a sheep, which suggests a pastoral herdsman. Chinese tradition describes the emperor Yu, founder of the first Hsia dynasty around 2000 B.C. as descended from the nomads. So apparently were the forebears of the Chou dynasty in the Feudal Age. Even more specifically, the ancestors of the Chin dynasty which ruled in the third century B.C. are legendarily held to have come from the region of Tibet. According to Chinese chroniclers the nomads, of whom the Tchiang constituted a considerable proportion, occupied from about 2000 B.C. to 60 B.C. a region covering Kansu, northern Szechwan, Shensi, and Shansi, and were independent of the Chinese. During the Han dynasty a Chinese general defeated the Tibetans for the first time in their own homeland. This was around 60 B.C. Thus for some two thousand years—if these legends are credible—the nomads who counted the Tibetans among them held the Chinese at bay and sometimes even attacked them.

With the decay of Han power the Tchiang again asserted themselves, and for over three hundred years, from 200 to 580 of the Christian era, the whole of north and northwest China was again in the hands of the nomadic peoples. It was only in the period of the Second Empire, covering the Sui and Tang dynasties from around 590 to 907, that the Chinese were able to dislodge the nomads, including the Tibetans, from the northern and northwest regions, the Tibetans being prised out of the Koko Nor area where they had established their rule.

This brings us to the historical period of the seventh century and to the reign of the great Song-tsan Gampo and of his father Nam-ri Song-tsan, who died in 630. The latter relaid the foundations of Tibetan independence by uniting the nomadic tribes and chieftains in Central Tibet, creating so prosperous a country that it was said that "the king built his palace with cement moistened with the milk of the cow and the yak." * It was Song-tsan Gampo who extended his sway over Ladakh in the west and the untamed Kiang tribes of the north. Moving south he conquered Nepal, penetrating the Himalayas into India where he established his rule in Bengal. Chinese historians, mentioning this period of Tibetan rule in India, which ended in the eleventh century with the dissolution of the Tibetan monarchy, describe the area ruled as the whole of Bengal up to the sea. The Bay of Bengal was christened the Tibetan Sea. Nepal rebelled, and recovered her independence in 703.

In the latter half of the eighth century Ti-Song Detsan, grandson of Song-tsan Gampo, was king of Tibet, and in his reign the country reached its zenith. "All the countries on the four frontiers were subdued," notes a Tibetan chronicler of this period. "China in the east, India in the south, Baltistan and Gilgit in the west, and Kashgar in the north were brought under his [Ti-Song Detsan's] power." His successor, Ral-pan-chan, consolidated his conquests. "The range of the Sro-long-shen mountains," † notes another chronicler, "resembling a curtain of white silk, was the frontier with the

---

* A squat, shaggy bull used mainly as a beast of burden at high altitudes in Tibet. The female of the species is sometimes referred to as *dri*.
† In eastern Tibet, now in China.

Chinese king of astrology. Near the great river Ganges, there was an iron pillar which was the frontier with the Indian king of religion. The gate of Pa-ta Shadung was the frontier with the Persian king of wealth, and the ridge of sand which looks like the back of Nya-mang-ma was the frontier of the king of Be-ta." Tibetans know the three kings, Song-tsan Gampo, Ti-Song Detsan and Ral-pa-chan as "The Three Religious Kings, Men of Power."

With Sino-Tibetan relations since then we have already dealt, but the more significant high-lights might be noted. Early in the thirteenth century the Mongol hordes of Genghiz Khan, as we saw, set out to conquer the world. The significant fact is that while the whole of the Chinese world up to Annam came under Mongol rule, Tibet alone was able not only to preserve her then ramshackle independence but to strengthen it by wooing Kublai Khan to Lamaism. The dissolution of the Mongol Empire was accompanied by the decline of Lamaism, which under the succeeding dynasty of the Mings suffered a further setback as the Ming emperors, unable to impose their direct authority on Tibet, attempted indirectly to retain their influence by playing off the lamas against one another and by encouraging secular leaders to come forward. This weakened Tibet internally but did not impair her independence. The extraordinary fact emerges that over 3,500 years, with a brief interlude during the Han dynasty, the Chinese were unable to assert their authority.

Even before the Mings collapsed to make way for the Manchus, Lamaism received a fresh lease of life in Mongolia and Tibet. History repeated itself, the Mongol chieftain Altan Khan being converted to Lamaism, as we saw, by the third Incarnate Lama Sonam Gyatse, who was thereupon invested with the title of Dalai Lama. Similarly the Great Fifth, as we have also noted, was later invested with sovereignty over Tibet by another Mongol chieftain, Gusri Khan.

These episodes vividly illustrate the resilience of the Tibetans, their will for freedom, and their willingness to fight in order to retain or achieve it.

The death in 1680 of the Great Fifth, which was kept secret for some ten years by the regent Sangye Gyatso, saw the rise of discord and dissension within Tibet. Taking advantage of this, the Manchus asserted their authority over Tibet, which for the next two centuries, until the dynasty's fall in 1911, was subject to Chinese control and direction. The details of these developments we have noted. From this account it would appear that from prehistoric days until 1951 the Tibetans have functioned as a free people for around 3,500 years with two interruptions, each of about two hundred years— the first during the Han dynasty and the second during the Manchu era. Although Tibet was part of Kublai Khan's domains, his conversion to Lamaism ensured its independence under the Sakya priest-kings.

Developments in China during the Manchu period affected the course of events in Tibet. Until about 1840, when the Manchus found themselves embroiled in the First Opium War with Britain and when China was increasingly exposed to the rapacity of foreign Powers, the Manchus held the reins of authority. By the end of the Second Opium War, in 1860, the power of China, as well as that of the Manchus, had waned, and Tibet found itself eyed with more than usual interest by certain foreign Powers, notably Britain and Russia.

Until then the interest of Western countries in the Hidden Land was exploratory and commercial. Some accounts name Friar Odoric of Pordenone as the first European to have reached Lhasa around 1328, but this is open to doubt. It is more likely that the first pioneer was the Portuguese Jesuit Antonio de Andrada (1580–1634) who, traveling from India, appears to have entered Tibet in the Manasarovar Lake region on the west. The first Europeans to enter Lhasa were two Jesuit priests, an Austrian named Grueber and a Belgian, D'Orville. They came from Peking in 1661, traveling by Lake Koko Nor to the Tibetan capital. Thereafter followed a long train of missionaries, explorers, and traders.

British interest in Tibet goes back to 1774 when George Bogle, a writer (or clerk) of the East India Company, was sent by Warren Hastings, first governor general of British India, to explore the possibilities of trade between Tibet and and the East India Company. Bogle visited Shigatse where he saw the then Tashi Lama,* now known as the Panchen Lama, who referred the British proposition to Peking, whence no more was heard. The Manchus were firmly in the saddle. Bogle's account is interesting. He mentions having observed among the treasures in the Panchen Lama's palace some goods from Russia, presumably transported from what is now the Buriat-Mongolian Republic of the U.S.S.R. In 1783 Hastings dispatched another envoy to Tibet, Captain Samuel Turner, who again got no farther than Shigatse, with the same negative result. The Chinese, unversed in the ways of Western diplomacy, traditionally regarded foreign envoys as mere bearers of tribute, and as such not entitled to be treated as equals. Turner was rebuffed, but from his account it would appear that the Chinese were also suspicious of British intentions in Tibet, particularly since Hastings' efforts followed a move against Bhutan, then a tributary of Tibet.† In 1772 the Bhutanese had invaded the principality of Cooch Behar in Bengal, which appealed to the British for aid. Hastings had then sent a force which drove out the invaders,

* He was at the time regent for Tibet.

† According to Bhutanese records Tibetan troops invaded the country at the end of the ninth century, "drove out the Indian princes and their subjects," and settled down in occupation of the land.

pursuing them into their own territory. At this juncture the Tashi Lama in his capacity as regent for Bhutan * intervened, and a treaty of peace was negotiated in 1774. In his account of his mission Turner refers to a letter sent by the Chinese amban in Lhasa to the Panchen Lama which clearly reflects the suspicions of the Chinese. Paraphrasing the amban's letter, Turner writes: "The *Ferenghi* [Westerners] were fond of war, and after insinuating themselves into a country raised disturbances and made themselves masters of it; and as no Ferenghis had ever been admitted to Tibet he advised the Tashi Lama to find some method of sending them back."

During the next hundred years Britain's interest was absorbed by the frontier areas of Sikkim and Bhutan, both of which were then tributaries of Tibet, and by Nepal. These three frontier states are adjacent to one another, with Sikkim bounded on the west by Nepal and on the east by Bhutan. The northern frontiers of all three abut on Tibetan territory, and all of them contain a number of Tibetans known as Bhotias. All have had associations with Lhasa.

After the peace treaty of 1774 British relations with Bhutan were marked by no incident until 1826 when the British occupied Assam. It was then discovered that the Bhutanese had usurped a tract of territory in Assam known as the Duars, and for this the British exacted an indemnity. The Bhutanese, however, failed to pay the tribute and resisted British demands for compensation. Relations deteriorated, and in 1863 the British sent an envoy to Bhutan to demand reparations for certain alleged "outrages," but the Bhutanese held him captive and forced him under duress to sign a treaty ceding the disputed territory to Bhutan. This treaty was repudiated by the British and an expedition dispatched. In

* Here is an early example of the Chinese efforts to invest the Tashi (or Panchen) Lama with political authority vis-à-vis the Dalai Lama.

November, 1865, Bhutan sued for peace, restored the disputed territory, and in return received an annual subsidy from the British Government which was later increased. In 1910 another treaty was concluded whereby the Bhutanese Government agreed to be guided in its external affairs by the British Government and the latter in turn undertook to exercise no interference in its internal affairs. It is worth noting that in the same year the Chinese Government formally claimed Bhutan as a feudatory; but the British, rejecting the demand, asserted that Bhutan was independent of China and that its external affairs were under the British Government. To this legacy, with all its commitments and responsibilities, the present independent Government of India has succeeded. Nor has the attitude of the present Communist Government of China changed. Communist Chinese maps today show Bhutan as part of China.

Sikkim's associations with Tibet are even closer than those of Bhutan, for its ruling family claim descent from one of the *gyalpos,* or princelings, of eastern Tibet, and Lamaism is the state religion. Until the end of the eighteenth century Sikkim was practically a dependency of Tibet, and its ruler was designated Governor of Sikkim. In 1816, at the end of the Nepalese-British War, to which we refer below, the *terrai,* or submontane, portion of Sikkim which the Nepalese had occupied was restored by the British to Sikkim's ruler but was taken back in 1849 as retaliation for certain injuries and insults inflicted on two British travelers who had been imprisoned by the Sikkimese. Relations with the British grew increasingly strained, and in 1861 came the usual show of force with the dispatch of British troops to Sikkim, which was obliged to sign a treaty "defining good relations." The Sikkimese, however, continued to be stubborn, the ruler spending most of his time in Tibet. In 1888 the British sent another expedition into Sikkim to eject some Tibetan soldiers who had built a fort there, and a convention was then signed in 1890 with China whereby the British protectorate over Sikkim was acknowledged and the boundary of the state defined. It is noteworthy that the Tibetans formally repudiated this treaty, thereby asserting their independence.

Nepal, like Bhutan and Sikkim, also has affinities with Tibet. Its people are of mixed Mongol origin and, besides the Bhotias or Tibetans, include many other races such as the Newars, Lepchas, and Gurkhas. The Gurkhas, a martial race, are descendants of the Brahmans and Rajputs who were driven out of India by the Moslems, took refuge in Nepal, and intermarried there. The state religion is Hinduism, and even the Buddhism that exists is so intermingled with and influenced by Hinduism as to be hardly recognizable.

Until the fall of the Manchus, Nepal maintained relations with China, occasionally sending an envoy with presents to Peking. From ancient days it has had commercial relations with Tibet, the principal trade routes being two— one running northeast from Katmandu to the frontier post of Nilam, crossing the Himalayan Range at a height of 14,000 feet; the other passing out of the northwest valley over the Himalayas into Tibet. The Kalimpong-Lhasa route has taken away much of the trade along these two trails.

Nepal has always regarded itself as independent both in its foreign relations and in its internal affairs, a status recognized by the British Government in December, 1923, though only after some shifts in relationships. This status is also recognized by the present independent Government of India. Within a period of some seventy years the Gurkhas of Nepal have twice invaded Tibet, but met with stout resistance, though they were successful on the second occasion. In 1788 the Gurkhas who had gained ascendancy in Nepal occupied some Tibetan districts near the Nepal frontier and three years later captured Shigatse. The Chinese thereupon sent reinforcements to the Tibetans, and a mixed Chinese-Tibetan force under Chinese generalship repulsed the Gurkhas, pursuing them to Noakote, a few miles from Katmandu, where the Chinese dictated terms to the Nepalese whereunder the latter were required to send tribute to Peking every fifth year. This was in 1792 when the Manchu dynasty had reached its apogee under the celebrated Emperor Chien Lung. The Chinese, perhaps justifiably, believed that the British had a hand in the Gurkha invasion, and the suspicion was probably well grounded, for in 1791 the Nepalese had entered into a commercial treaty with the British, who, after the Gurkha reverse, had sent their representative, Colonel Kirkpatrick, to Noakote. Kirkpatrick, however, arrived only after the conclusion of peace, but managed to extricate another commercial treaty in Britain's favor from the chastened Nepalese.

The Chinese reaction to these events is interesting. They closed Tibet as far as possible to foreign influences, and decreed that all foreign questions should be dealt with by the ambans, and not by the Tibetan Government. All foreigners in Tibet were henceforth suspect. Chien Lung died in 1795, and with his passing the power of the Manchu dynasty and of China rapidly declined. Simultaneously Western interference and intrigue in both China and Tibet intensified. In 1850, following the visit of Jung Bahadur, ruler of Nepal, to Britain, Nepalese-British ties grew stronger, and five years later the Gurkhas were again emboldened to invade Tibet. The Manchus, irked by multiple foreign infiltration into China, were in no position to help. Nine years earlier the Tibetans, faced by an invasion of Dogras from Kashmir, had dealt with the intruders effectively, almost exterminating them, but the Nepalese posed a more formidable threat. The Tibetans were forced to sue for peace, and the resultant treaty secured for Nepal extraterritorial rights, the establishment of an agency in Lhasa and other centers, an annual subsidy of 10,000 rupees (now equivalent to $2,000), and the right of free trade with Tibet.

Had it not been for the Indian Mutiny of 1857, it is possible that the British might have attempted to peer closely into Tibet earlier than they did. The Ming period in China saw an influx of European voyagers and traders, beginning in the sixteenth century. The Portuguese, French, Dutch, and British opened trade with China, and in 1784 the first ship from the United States entered Chinese waters. In 1669 China signed her first treaty with a European power, Russia, and between 1839 and 1860 the two opium wars and a long series of foreign treaties took place, crippling China and leaving her the victim of rival imperialisms. By 1860 the Manchus were at their last gasp.

In 1876 Britain exacted from China as the annex to a treaty the right to send an official to Tibet on what was euphemistically described as "scientific exploration." If the enervated Manchus were pliant the Tibetans were not, and it sheds a revealing light on Chinese claims to sovereignty over Tibet that the Tibetan Government refused to permit the entry of a British official into Tibet. The Chinese had no alternative to withdrawing a concession which they had nominal authority to give but no real authority to enforce.

Tibetan suspicion of British intentions had earlier been aroused by the dispatch from 1863 onward of surveying spies who were Indians for the most part but who also included a few Tibetans. The best known of these was Pandit Nain Singh who entered Tibet in the disguise of a merchant from Ladakh. He carried a prayer wheel in which a compass was secreted, and his 108-bead rosary served his survey purposes, for he dropped a bead with every hundred paces he took. Nain Singh entered Tibet twice, the first time in 1866 and again eight years later. Another Indian to enter Tibet on behalf of the British was the well-known Pandit Krishna (called A.K.) who visited Lhasa in 1878, staying there for about a year. A Tibetan from Sikkim, U-gyen Gya-tso, was also employed by the British, and he was instrumental in securing the permission of the authorities of the Tashi-lhunpo monastery for an Indian, Sarat Chandra Das, to enter Tibet as a student. In this guise Das made a series of exploratory journeys inside Tibet, bringing back, besides much valuable information, a large number of books in Tibetan and Sanskrit. When the Tibetans discovered the real character of these explorations, particularly those of Das, they were incensed and took even more stringent precautions against the entry of foreigners. In 1892 an Englishman, Lieutenant Colonel L. Austin Wadell, who attempted to reach Lhasa from the Nepal side in the disguise of a Tibetan pilgrim, was summarily bundled out of the country.

Although the Tibetans refused in 1890 to accept the Sino-British treaty whereby Sikkim became a British protectorate —the Tibetans insisted it was still feudatory to them—they were unable to enforce their repudiation of the treaty nor were the Manchus in any position to assist them. The 1890 treaty had stipulated for the opening of a trade mart at Yatung and for the entry of duty-free imports from India into Tibet. Compelled to comply with these provisions, the Tibetan attitude to the British grew more and more recalcitrant. The thirteenth Dalai Lama was now on the Golden Throne, and as Manchu authority waned he embarked on a policy of preserving Tibet's *de facto* independence by playing off the Russians against the British and the Chinese against both. Faced with British hostility and suspicion, he leaned more heavily on the Chinese and the Russians. Communications addressed by the British Government to the Dalai Lama were returned unopened on the plea that His Holiness could only receive letters from foreign Powers through the ambans.

The first Slav to enter Tibet was the explorer Prjewalsky, who is described as a Russian though his name sounds Polish. He traveled a great deal in northern Tibet, the last of his four journeys taking place between November, 1883, and October, 1885. In the course of his travels Prjewalsky studied closely the topography of the northeastern and eastern mountain systems, making an intensive investigation of the Tsaidam Basin. It is these areas that have always interested Russia most, just as in China proper Moscow's eyes have been focused on Outer Mongolia and on Sinkiang which abuts on Tibet and Kashmir. China's relationship with Outer Mongolia, which until the Communist advent was for all practical purposes independent, was similar to its relationship with Tibet. Outer Mongolia's natural orientation was through the Trans-Siberian railway to the U.S.S.R., but the Sino-Soviet treaty of 1924 recognized that "Outer Mongolia is an integral part of the Republic of China and respects China's sovereignty therein." Tsarist Russia, however, with other European countries was anxious to have its slice of the Chinese melon, and in 1898 China was forced to recognize the territory north of the Great Wall as a Russian "sphere of interest." The British with their Indian Empire were naturally wary of Russian moves in China and Tibet.

In the opening years of the twentieth century there appeared on the Tibetan scene a mysterious individual referred to as "the Russian agent" Dorjieff. He seems to have been a lama hailing from Buriat-Mongolia, and his arrival in Tibet aroused acute British suspicion. Being of the Lamaist faith, Dorjieff received a warm welcome in Tibet. In 1903 Russia's incursions into Manchuria had disturbed the Japanese, and relations between the two countries deteriorated.

They were to erupt in the following year in the Russo-Japanese War.

To the British this seemed an opportune moment for moving against Tibet. On the plea that the Tibetans and Chinese were stalling with the British while intriguing with the Russians, the British in December, 1903, dispatched a military force to open a way into Tibet for a mission headed by Colonel (later Sir Francis) Younghusband. China was too feeble to render any effective aid. The Tibetans, in the words of some foreign observers, "were shot down like partridges." Younghusband entered Lhasa in August, 1904. A large insect, as the Tibetans put it, had eaten a small insect. Younghusband discovered that the Dalai Lama with his entourage had fled to Mongolia, but he negotiated a treaty with the Tibetan delegates which in effect virtually made Tibet a British sphere of influence. Henceforth, it was ordained, no Tibetan territory could be ceded or leased to any foreign Power without previous British consent. Never was China's prestige in Tibet so low.

The Dalai Lama who returned to Tibet in 1909 entertained no great respect for the Chinese, who during his exile had compelled him to kowtow before the Imperial Throne at Peking, where he was condescendingly dismissed by the emperor with the title of "Loyally Submissive Vice Regent." Even while on his way back reports reached His Holiness of various aggressive acts by the Chinese in Tibet. After signing the Lhasa Convention the British had withdrawn their forces, thereby creating a vacuum into which the Chinese stepped. Enraged by their own impotence and the unconcealed contempt of the Tibetans, the Imperial Government in Peking had sent an army to Tibet accompanied by an official to reimpose Chinese authority. The army was commanded by General Chao Erh-feng, whose entry was resisted by the Tibetans. Feng Chien, the Chinese deputy amban, was assassinated. In retaliation General Chao's troops destroyed several monasteries and were ruthless in suppressing the revolt. Chao anticipated the Communists by inaugurating schemes for having the land cultivated by Chinese immigrants, depriving the monasteries of their secular powers, limiting the number of lamas, and replacing Tibetan magistrates by Chinese.

Meanwhile the Dalai Lama had returned to Lhasa to find the Chinese ensconced firmly in authority. His Holiness soon found himself at loggerheads with the Chinese amban Lien Yu. As the Manchus' enfeebled grip relaxed on China, their attitude to the Tibetans grew more vengeful. The Dalai Lama was forced to flee again—this time to Darjeeling in India where the British authorities accorded him great consideration. There is a curious parallel between the events which followed the thirteenth Dalai Lama's flight to India in February, 1910, and the flight of the fourteenth Dalai Lama nearly fifty years later. Then as now the Chinese troops overwhelmed the Tibetans and ruthlessly restored order. The Chinese amban at Lhasa took all power into his hands, the Tibetan ministers being reduced to a status of servility. Meanwhile, according to Sir Charles Bell,* the Government of China informed the British minister at Peking "that they had no intention of altering the administration of Tibet, still less of converting it into a province, which, as they were careful to point out, would be a contravention of treaties. Both promises," notes Bell dryly, "were soon to be broken." Then as now the Chinese Government sought the return of the Dalai Lama to Tibet. Soon after His Holiness's flight Peking made overtures to the British

* In his book *Tibet: Past and Present* (Oxford University Press, 1924). Sir Charles, who is rated the foremost British authority on Tibet, served for some time as British representative at Lhasa.

Government in India, inviting it to induce the Dalai Lama to return. On this move Sir Charles Bell's comment is interesting: "It would have suited the Chinese book to keep him [the Dalai Lama] as a State prisoner, and, if harsher measures were necessary, it would have been easy to adopt them. But to such betrayal our government declined to agree and the idea was accordingly abandoned. Had it been followed, there would have been an end of the Dalai Lama." On subsequent developments—on the collapse of the Manchu dynasty, the return of the Dalai Lama, the ejection of the Chinese from Tibet, and the Dalai Lama's declaration of Tibet's independence we have briefly dwelt.*

Between the Lhasa Convention of 1904, following the Younghusband expedition, and the Dalai Lama's proclamation of Tibet's independence in 1912, several interesting developments occurred, to which we have also referred. In 1906 China by the Peking Convention confirmed the Lhasa Convention, but the very fact that the British Government sought Chinese approval of their treaty with Tibet was an implied recognition of the special relationship between China and Tibet. What was that relationship? The St. Petersburg Convention of 1907 between Britain and Russia gave it a name. For the first time the term "suzerain" was employed to describe the relationship between China and Tibet. By this convention Britain and Russia recognized Chinese authority over Tibet and stipulated that neither Britain nor Russia should interfere in the internal administration of that country. They also bound themselves not to seek concessions there or take any part of the revenue or depute representatives to Lhasa.

The motivations which induced the signing of the convention were probably similar on both sides. Britain and Russia were each anxious that the other should not secure too pre-

* See Chapter Two.

dominant a place in China, and if the convention ensured this in Tibet it served the purposes of both Powers.* Tibet has a strategic situation, its high plateaus dominating India; moreover, both parties were well aware of the Dalai Lama's spiritual influence in Manchuria and Mongolia. So were the Chinese. Within a year of the St. Petersburg Convention they implemented their suzerainty by seizing administrative power in Tibet, bringing in troops and forcing the Dalai Lama to flee to India in 1910. The fall of the Manchus, the return of the Dalai Lama to Lhasa, and his proclamation of Tibet's independence called for a reevaluation of the situation.

This the British proceeded to do by inaugurating a tripartite conference at Simla in October, 1913, to which they invited Chinese and Tibetan representatives. Here, as we have seen, the Tibetans were persuaded by the British to accept Chinese suzerainty in return for Peking's assurance that Tibet would be internally autonomous. Tibet, for administrative purposes, was divided into Outer Tibet, containing Lhasa, Shigatse, and Chamdo, and Inner Tibet, the area adjoining China which includes Bitang, Litang, Tachienlu and a large portion of eastern Tibet. The terms Outer and Inner are applied to Tibet as seen from China much as the same labels are applied to Mongolia. As far as Outer Tibet was concerned, its autonomy was recognized; China undertook not to interfere in its administration, and to refrain from sending troops and officials there; not to establish a Chinese colony nor to require Tibet to be represented in the Chinese Parliament. The Chinese delegates at the conference agreed to these terms, but Peking refused to ratify the convention following differences on what constituted the boundary line between Inner and Outer Tibet. Peking laid a claim to Chamdo, Litang, and Batang in Outer Tibet which

* As a result of the Bolshevik Revolution this convention is believed to be no longer in force.

the Tibetans resisted. Since the Chinese failed to ratify the treaty, the Tibetan plea is that this absolved Lhasa from its recognition of Chinese suzerainty.

In various ways since then, until the Chinese Communists imposed their control, the Tibetans have attempted to assert their independence. During the First World War they offered to send a thousand soldiers to fight alongside Britain, an index to their increasingly friendly feelings toward that country. China, meanwhile, was disrupted by civil war, and the authority of the Central Government did not extend to the outlying areas. Seizing the opportunity, a Chinese garrison commander on the Sino-Tibetan border in the east attacked the Tibetans but was repulsed by them. The incident occurred in 1917, and is related by Sir Eric Teichman,* who was then the British consular agent in Tibet. Not only did the Tibetans repulse the Chinese but they also recaptured certain areas of Tibetan territory previously annexed by the Chinese. Teichman's intervention secured a truce. In his opinion had the fighting continued, "another month or so would possibly have seen several thousand more Chinese prisoners in Tibetan hands and the Lhasa force in possession of all the country up to Tachienlu." Tachienlu is on the border between eastern Tibet and China, and on the main route between the two countries.

In the Tibetan view, the sentimental and religious bonds which existed between China and Tibet were broken by the Chinese revolution of 1911. "Tibet thereafter," according to the Tibetan appeal to the United Nations in November, 1950, "depended entirely on her isolation, her faith in the wisdom of the Lord Buddha, and occasionally on the support of the British in India for protection." From 1912 onward Tibet maintained independent relations with neighboring

* In his book *Travels of a Consular Officer in Eastern Tibet* (Cambridge University Press, 1922).

countries such as India and Nepal. In this period the Tibetan Government conducted its own foreign affairs, maintained its own army, had its own coinage, and controlled its internal administration. In the Second World War Tibet did not compromise her position by throwing in her forces on the side of China, and in 1942, when the Kuomintang Government pressed for the opening of communications through Tibet, Lhasa successfully resisted the claim. Until the Chinese Communist invasion all officials and other functionaries in the country were appointed by Lhasa independently of the Chinese Government. Indeed, it would not be incorrect to say that in this period Tibet had closer relations with India than with China, both when India was under British rule and when in August, 1947, it became independent.

When the Nationalist Government ruled China several attempts were made to reassert China's authority in Tibet, but all of them were consistently rebuffed. In 1933 Chiang Kai-shek sent a mission to Lhasa calling on the Tibetan Government to let China handle its foreign affairs and share in its internal administration. The Tibetans refused. They also declared that they would not recognize Chinese suzerainty unless certain frontier territory inhabited by a majority of Tibetans was ceded to Tibet. This is interesting in view of the present Dalai Lama's declaration of June 20, 1959, that not only must Tibet return to her pre-1950 status but that the disputed areas on her northern and eastern frontiers should be given back to her. His Holiness was alluding to the Tibetan-inhabited regions of Chinghai and western Szechwan, possibly also to Kansu, though he made no specific reference to any area.

In 1939 the Chinese Nationalist Government tried again, and again failed. Thereafter the Sino-Japanese War absorbed China's attention, and in this difficult period relations between China and Tibet improved, though in 1942 the Nationalist Government refused to have any dealings with the newly established Tibetan Foreign Affairs Bureau which the Communists were later summarily to demolish. To other efforts by Nationalist China we have previously referred, but late in 1945 a Tibetan mission visited China and asked for the recognition of Tibet's independence and for the return of all Tibetan territory occupied by the Chinese. To Chiang Kai-shek, who had categorically proclaimed that "the frontiers of China lie in Tibet," this request was inadmissible. It was also the Nationalist Government which by its announcement in 1944 that a new Panchen Lama had been found and enthroned in Chinghai—despite Tibetan protests—put a powerful weapon later in the hands of the Chinese Communists. The Panchen Lama whom the Chinese Nationalists hoped to exploit is now being exploited by the Communists.

Between the end of the First World War and the beginning of the Second, Tibet moved closer within the British orbit. In 1921 Sir Charles Bell, who since 1908 had handled British relations with Tibet, Bhutan, and Sikkim, was recalled from retirement and sent again to Lhasa as head of a diplomatic mission. Its object, as Bell subsequently revealed in his book *Portrait of the Dalai Lama,** was to persuade Tibet to accept British arms, allow Britain to train Tibetan troops as well as munitions workers who would turn out explosives and rifles, accept British mining prospectors and machinery, and allow an English-teaching school to be opened at Gyantse with a British headmaster. Mainly with the support of the wealthy and influential Tsarong Dzasa, who though born a commoner rose to be commander in chief of the Tibetan Army and one of the thirteenth Dalai Lama's principal advisers, Bell was able to persuade the Tibetans to agree in principle to his proposals. Tsarong lived to see the Communists come in but did not long survive the Red

* Cambridge University Press, 1945.

regime. He had been instrumental as commander in chief in defeating the Chinese troops in the revolution of 1911 and forcing them out of Tibet. In the previous year when the thirteenth Dalai Lama fled to India pursued by Chinese troops, Tsarong, with a handful of soldiers and monks, had held up the Chinese pursuers at the Chaksam ferry on the river Tsangpo and enabled His Holiness to escape. When the fourteenth Dalai Lama fled to India in March, 1959, Tsarong, by then a man of seventy-two, courageously decided to stay behind in Lhasa. His death was reported not long afterward. Apparently he committed suicide after being publicly beaten by some of his servants and a few pro-Chinese monks and humiliated before his people. This is one of the methods by which the Chinese Communists attempt to denigrate and dispose of Tibetan dignitaries opposed to them.

With Bell's departure from Tibet in 1921, Lhasa showed a shift in relations. By 1925 the thirteenth Dalai Lama seemed to be moving away from the British orbit to the Chinese. What His Holiness was really engaged in doing was attempting to maintain Tibet's *de facto* independence by playing off the Chinese against the British. The Russians, after the Bolshevik Revolution, having voluntarily relinquished their extraterritorial rights in China no longer represented a threat to Tibet. The Dalai Lama's Government had also always resented the British Government's acceptance of the concept of Chinese suzerainty over Tibet.

What the concept of suzerainty exactly implies has long been a matter of dispute among international jurists. The Tibetan view was stated in Tibet's appeal to the United Nations in November, 1950. "There were times," this appeal declared, "when Tibet sought, but seldom received, the protection of the Chinese Empire. The Chinese, however, in their natural urge for expansion, have wholly misconstrued the significance of the ties of friendship and interdependence that existed between China and Tibet as between neighbors. To them China was a suzerain and Tibet a vassal state. It is this which aroused legitimate apprehension in the mind of Tibet regardless of the designs of China on her independent status. . . . The Chinese claim Tibet as a part of China. Tibetans feel that racially, culturally, and geographically they are apart from the Chinese. The conquest of Tibet by China will only enlarge the area of conflict and increase the threat to the independence of other Asian countries."

The Chinese have laid claim not only to suzerainty but to sovereignty, insisting that Tibet is an integral part of Chinese territory and that Tibetan borders are Chinese borders. When the Tibetan appeal came before the United Nations, the Kuomintang Chinese delegate Mr. Liu stated that "Tibet had been part of China for seven hundred years, and all Chinese, whatever their party or religion, regarded it as such." Mr. Liu, however, referred to Sun Yat-sen's declaration affirming the equality of the five branches of the Chinese race —the Han, Manchu, Mongolian, Hui, and Tibetan. He recalled that the representatives of Tibet had taken part in drafting the new Chinese constitution in 1946 and in electing the president and vice president of the Republic in 1947; but he also recalled that Sun Yat-sen had stated that "if disputes arose between those branches they should never be settled by force." The Kuomintang condemned the Communists for settling the dispute by force.

Britain's attitude, as we have seen, was equivocal and sometimes inconsistent. The British were prepared to treat the Tibetans as "gentlemen" but not to recognize their independence in principle, though they conceded it in practice. They realized that the Lhasa Government was virtually independent and that Chinese sovereignty was only technically maintained. But they were reluctant to say so openly. Hence they sought a compromise, simultaneously persuading the

Russians, Chinese, and Tibetans to accept it by supporting the principle of Tibet's internal independence within the orbit of Chinese suzerainty. Peking, as we have seen, refused to ratify the Simla Convention; consequently Tibet resiled from her earlier acceptance. Suzerainty was left dangling like a floating kidney in the Sino-Tibetan body politic. Independent India had a chance between 1947 and 1949, when the Chinese National Government was on its way out and when the Communists were not yet in, to recognize Tibet as an independent sovereign state and thereby secure a buffer region between China and herself. Unfortunately she chose to inherit the British legacy and to recognize the Chinese Government as the suzerain authority in Tibet.

What exactly does suzerainty imply? As we noted, it is a juristic concept which eludes precise definition and has been more often than not described in negative terms. Originally the word "suzerain" was one of feudal law where the vassal owed certain duties to the feudal lord and the lord in turn was bound to perform certain reciprocal duties. It was therefore even in its pristine form a two-way obligation. In modern times suzerainty has come to be used as descriptive of relations, vague and ill defined, which exist between powerful and dependent states. But a state under suzerainty is different from a protectorate. In the latter case there is a diminution of the sovereignty of a protected state, whereas in the case of suzerainty there is a reduction in the sovereignty of the dominant state. Where suzerainty exists the vassal state has larger powers of action than those belonging to a protected state, since suzerainty proceeds from a concession by the suzerain. There is reciprocity of obligation, and the vassal state acquires certain of the powers of an independent country, which might extend to the conferring of its exequatur on foreign consuls or the making of commercial conventions. As subject to suzerain authority, a vassal state cannot normally conclude treaties unless specifically empowered to do so by its suzerain.

The character of suzerainty has varied greatly, and its very ambiguity has been exploited, this being its main recommendation to imperialists in a hurry or in difficulties. Suzerainty might be nominal, as it was in feudal times when the Papacy held Naples in fief. Or it might be real, as it was in the case of the Ottoman Empire and Egypt. The sign of vassalship is the acceptance and approval by the suzerain power of the individual who heads the internal government of the subordinate state. China attempted to do this in the case of the Dalai Lama in Tibet, but with no great success except at intermittent intervals under the Manchus.

The international status of a vassal state under suzerainty is again ambiguous, one reason why another state, in this case El Salvador, had to sponsor Tibet's case against China before the United Nations in 1950. In the opinion of the celebrated international jurist Dr. L. Oppenheim, a vassal state which has absolutely no relations whatever with other states is "a half-sovereign State." But Tibet does not fall into this category, since at various times she has had relations with other states, and China's suzerainty is itself a matter of reciprocal obligation where a lapse on the part of the suzerain authority releases the vassal state from its obligation.

This is the core of Tibet's contention against China.

han
imperialism

CHAPTER SEVEN

With China's forcible seizure of Tibet the Communist Chinese have come to the straggling 2,000-mile-long Indian frontier running from Ladakh in Kashmir to the eastern fringes of the Northeast Frontier Agency, and including within it the 500-mile frontier of Nepal. Until 1959 Tibet, "the highest country in the world," with its bleak desolate northern tracts, and ringed by the Himalayas to the south, provided an ideal buffer state between India and China. So long as China did not dominate the uplands, the valleys, and the plains leading through the Himalayan passes to India, Tibet offered an effective barrier. Shut off by geography and partly by design from the outer world, Tibet had for centuries lived a conservative feudal existence, suspicious of foreigners and eager to maintain her independence and way of life.

All this has now changed. From a buffer state Tibet has become a potential springboard, and the Chinese dragon may well take its long leap forward into Southeast Asia from there. In the vulnerable areas of Ladakh, Nepal, Bhutan, Sikkim, and in some districts of NEFA, reside many people religiously and racially akin to the Tibetans. The Chinese, who now control the Tibetans, can use them as instruments of political infiltration into the regions which cartographically they already claim. Under the shadow of the new dispensation on the Indo-Tibetan border, foreign and defense policies must change, for behind these frontier regions is the great land mass of India with Pakistan and Burma to the west and east and, beyond, the polyglot countries of Southeast Asia, with a considerable Chinese population. The Himalayan region might prove to be the cockpit of the world.

The construction by the Communists of two major highways in China—others are being planned—not only links Tibet closer with China but makes the Indo-Tibetan frontier more accessible to motor-truck traffic coming from China and Tibet. Since 1951 the Chinese have also been busy constructing military bases and airfields in southern Tibet. Henceforward the Han colonization of Tibet will be intensified, converting Tibet within a few years into a Chinese settlement with a preponderating Chinese majority.

To appreciate better and to assess more accurately the danger and threat which these activities pose, the real nature of Communist Chinese policy toward the national minorities should be understood. Although these minorities, according to the 1953 Chinese census, number only 35 million (roughly 6 per cent of the population) they are spread over areas covering 60 per cent of the country. The frontier province of Sinkiang, or Chinese Turkestan, to the north of Tibet is one-sixth of all China. The largest minority are the Chuangs, who number over six million and who live mostly in Kwangsi Province; other minorities include the Uighurs (3.6 million) of the northwest; the Hui, or Chinese Moslems (3.5 million); the Yi (3.2 million), who reside largely in Yunnan; and the Mongols (1.4 million), living mainly in Inner Mongolia. The Chinese estimate the number of Tibetans at 2.7 million, though a recent article in the *Peo-*

*ple's Daily** of Peking places their total at 1,200,000. Communist Chinese statistics are notoriously resilient and elastic. Of these minorities only the Hui speak Chinese.

Though the areas occupied by the national minorities are generally designated as autonomous, in practice the Chinese through the local Communist party branch, which is controlled by the National Council at Peking, have consistently attempted to consolidate centralized rule while keeping up the pretense of regional autonomy. Among the autonomous areas are Tibet, Inner Mongolia, Ningsia, and Kwangsi. The Communists have made a great show of their impartiality by condemning at times the sin of "Great Han Chauvinism," though simultaneously they stress that the Hans constitute "the overwhelming majority of the population and the main revolutionary force." On these grounds, the Communists explain their colonization tactics by stating that it is therefore necessary to send Han personnel into the national minority areas. Incidentally the Chuangs, who are the largest minority, are outnumbered almost three to one in Kwangsi. In these autonomous regions the Han cadres play down the differences between the national minority and the ruling race, and highlight the class differences among the former. They thus attempt to divide the minorities within themselves and at the same time draw them closer to the ruling Han race.

Land reform met initially with considerable resistance among the nomads of Sinkiang and Inner Mongolia, where the herd owners slaughtered their livestock rather than surrender them to the Communists, who were thereby compelled to go slow. In many areas the Han cadres had no alternative to winking at local feudal practices such as slave ownership, concubinage, and even human sacrifices, which for a time were permitted among the primitive Kawas. But ulti-

* Issue of May 6, 1959.

mately, under the guise of "democratic reforms," the minorities were brought to heel.

In some respects Tibet offered a tougher problem. Of all the non-Chinese races the Tibetans are the most nationalistic, and among the minority areas Tibet was closest to Mongolia, to whom in pre-Communist days she was accustomed to turning when Britain or Russia failed her against China. Mongolia lies to the northeast of Tibet, divided from that region only by a strip of the Chinese province of Kansu which the two separated regions claim is inhabited largely by Tibetans and Mongols. On the Chinese mainland Mongolia is Tibet's natural ally, each being closely related to the other in race, religion, and outlook. Urga is the capital of Mongolia, and the Grand Lama of Urga, head of the Mongolian church, has invariably been a Tibetan. Inner and Outer Tibet, as we have noted,* have their counterparts in Inner and Outer Mongolia.

In Mongolia as in Tibet the Communist Chinese encountered strong opposition to their "democratic reforms" and were compelled to go slow. In both areas separatist tendencies were strong, and both resisted the infiltration of Chinese settlers and were particularly afraid of assimilation. Their opposition to Communism, apart from the fact that it sought to undermine their religion and way of life, stemmed from the fact that Communist party leadership meant Chinese leadership. Neither Tibet nor Mongolia wanted to be absorbed, nor did the other so-called autonomous areas.

But all, of course, are now being rapidly absorbed and assimilated into the great family of Han imperialism. In the minority areas "Great Han Chauvinism" was initially condemned by the Communists, but this appeasement campaign was soon abandoned in favor of an all-out drive against "local nationalism." Significantly, one of the main features

* This division was made at the Simla Conference of 1914.

of the drive was a new migration of Chinese, from the over-crowded regions of North China and the Yangtse plains to the northwest, to Sinkiang, Chinghai, to the Khamba areas of West Szechwan (formerly the province of Sikang), and to Chamdo in Tibet. This assimilation drive, as we saw, lit a fire in northeast Tibet which finally reached Lhasa, enveloping almost the whole of Outer Tibet and large areas of Inner Tibet. The flames still flicker.

At his press conference at Mussoorie on June 20, 1959, the Dalai Lama claimed that the revolt was still going on and that "several places in the east and north of Lhasa" were still under the control of the Khambas who were Tibetans. At the time of the Dalai Lama's flight the Khambas, as we noted, also controlled a corridor running south of the Tsangpo to the Indian border along which the God-king made his way to India. The final outcome of this one-sided struggle, however, was never in doubt, for the Chinese aim was not only the armed suppression and political subjugation of Tibet but also its extinction as a separate civilization represented by a distinctive language, culture, religion, and government. This involved genocide and the suppression of human rights.

Because the Chinese Communists refused to allow an International Commission to visit Tibet to investigate the charges of Chinese crimes, an International Commission of Jurists was set up on a nonpolitical, nongovernmental basis at Geneva. This distinguished body, comprising twenty-two members drawn from different countries, is headed by Mr. Joseph T. Thorson, of Canada, and is representative of over thirty thousand lawyers in fifty countries. At the initiative of the commission its general secretary, Purshottam Trikamdas, a senior advocate of the Supreme Court of India, was deputed to make a preliminary inquiry and report. Trikamdas, who was assisted by a team of Indian experts, conducted his inquiry for two months, examining "reliable witnesses from

Tibet" and sifting through a mass of documents and materials, including press and radio reports, both Chinese and Indian. The report, released early in June and published the following month, constitutes a formidable indictment of the Peking regime.

"From 1912 to 1950," states Trikamdas, "there was no Chinese law [in Tibet], no Chinese judge, no Chinese policeman on the street corner; there was no Chinese newspaper, no Chinese soldier, and even no representative of the Chinese Government." The report then covers the developments following the Chinese occupation and culminating in the Tibetan rebellion of 1959. It describes the large-scale Chinese immigration into Tibet, particularly in the northeast and eastern areas, and estimates, "according to reliable sources," that about five million Chinese have already been settled in Tibet.* The report refers to the building of the new roads and highways with Tibetan labor involving some 200,000 men, women, children, laymen and monks, "many of them forcibly drafted for the work." Of this number, about one-fourth are said to have died of cold, hunger, and fatigue. From 1952 a policy of systematic destruction of religious freedom and persecution of monks was instituted. In Khan Province alone, 250 monasteries were destroyed. Of seven leading lamas charged with offenses "which fit into the general scheme of attack on religion," only one—Zongsar Khentse Rimpoche—escaped to India, the others being executed or imprisoned. Several heads of monasteries were killed, jailed, or publicly humiliated. "One case in our files," notes the report, "refers to a very highly respected lama who was stripped and dragged with a rope over a rocky terrain, as a result of which he died. . . . Cases have been reported of

* The report quotes the Dalai Lama as estimating the number of Chinese immigrants who had arrived in Tibet, or were being sent there, at nine million.

Head Lamas being dragged to death by horses, and a fairly large number sent as prisoners to concentration camps in China."

Coming to the rebellion of 1959 the report observes that large-scale aerial bombing was resorted to, since ground troops could not be extensively employed against the rebels in mountainous terrain. Reliable estimates of the number killed are about 65,000.* Another 20,000 are believed to have been deported, and after the suppression of the rising in Lhasa all Tibetan males from the ages of fifteen to sixty were removed from the capital to an unknown destination. The report recommends full investigation into the "alleged deportation of 20,000 Tibetan children." It was apparently not uncommon for high personages, suspected to be hostile to the Chinese, to be invited to parties by the Chinese military commanders, who then ordered them to be imprisoned or executed—a fact which impelled the Dalai Lama's advisers to counsel him against accepting an invitation to come to the Chinese military headquarters in Lhasa unescorted.

Trikamdas' report, which covers two hundred pages, was submitted to the commission which appointed him, and it was decided to set up a Legal Inquiry Committee in Tibet to collect further evidence for a more detailed report which will be submitted to the United Nations. "What at the moment appears to be attempted genocide," the report had warned, "may become the full act of genocide unless prompt and adequate action is taken." The Legal Inquiry Committee will continue to collect documents, and obtain interviews, commentaries, and statements for a final report to determine whether the crime of genocide is established. If it is, the commission will initiate action to refer the charge to the United Nations under the Genocide Convention of 1948 and the United Nations Charter itself. Several distinguished

* The Dalai Lama placed the figure higher but gave no specific total.

legal luminaries, including Lord Hartley Shawcross, former attorney general in Britain, and lawyers from India, Burma, Malaya, Ghana, Thailand, and the Philippines, have accepted membership on the committee whose first meeting is scheduled to be held in Delhi.

The Hans who swallowed up the Manchus are now ready to ingest the 35 million who constitute their national minorities. They have already done so in Inner Mongolia, in Sinkiang, Ningsia, Kansu, Chinghai, Szechwan, Kweichow, Yunnan, and Kwangsi. Tibet cannot for long survive the swoop of the dragon. Though pockets of resistance continue to the north and east of Lhasa, the back of the Tibetan rebellion has been broken as it was bound to be against the overwhelming superiority of numbers and equipment of the Chinese. According to the latter, the rebels numbered 20,000 of whom about one-third were Khambas. The Chinese Communists as far back as May were boasting that "the rebellion was utterly routed in the twinkling of an eye, in spite of the national and religious signboards held up by the rebels, the difficult terrain with high mountains and precipitous valleys and the many different kinds of foreign aid they got." The boast was premature; but events since then suggest that Tibet, like the other national minority areas, will soon be bound hand and foot to the chariot wheels of Communist China. "The fusion of one nationality with another," declared a Red spokesman, "is an inevitable process of historical development which no nationality can avoid."

The Khambas are good guerrilla fighters but so are the Chinese, particularly the Communist legions trained over the years by Mao Tse-tung and Chu Teh. They proved it in Korea against superior equipment and force. Those who have fought the Tibetans, including the British, have testified to their valor in battle. Writing of the Younghusband expedition, Sir Charles Bell observes: "The bravery of the Tibetans

came as a surprise to their opponents, but they had no military training and were in the main armed with antiquated
muzzle-loaders locally made. Neither these, nor the swords
that they carried, were of any use against modern firearms."
It is possible that against the Communists the Tibetans were
armed with more modern weapons than flintlocks and
muzzle-loaders. But the odds were immeasurably against
them.

Early in August, Nepalese border forces intercepted fleeing
Khamba remnants from Tibet, survivors of a group which
had fought a strong Chinese unit on the southern bank of the
Tsangpo River while the Dalai Lama headed southeast. They
had suffered heavy losses but had managed for nearly four
months to remain inside Tibet, harassing stray Chinese forces
until they were compelled to take refuge in Nepalese territory northeast of Katmandu in the Everest region. A Nepalese
unit keeping vigil on the border intercepted and disarmed
them. They asked to be sent to India and were sent across
the Indo-Nepalese border. Their number was not disclosed,
but with some five thousand Khambas already in India it
would seem that a considerable proportion of these guerrilla
fighters who resisted the Chinese are outside Tibet.

While the system of ruthless assimilation proceeds inside
Tibet and the national minorities are being absorbed according to the "inevitable process of historical development," the
Chinese Communists are by no means inactive outside their
national boundaries. As compared with the 35 million minority peoples inside China, there are 14 million Overseas Chinese who over the past thirty years have been wooed in turn
by the Kuomintang and the Communists. Although many of
them are strongly opposed to the Communist regime—and
these include a large proportion of those who left China for
that reason—a substantial number are inclined to Peking.
The vast majority of them are inclined to favor Peking and

constitute the Chinese Communists' shock brigades in the countries of Southeast Asia. Though divided by a dozen national boundaries, they are influential within individual countries and regions ranging from Burma and Singapore to Malaya, Thailand, Indonesia, and the Philippines. In recent years the propagandist activities of the *hua-ch'iao*, as the Overseas Chinese are called, has been curbed in the last three countries. At the Bandung Conference in the summer of 1955, Chou En-lai tried to pose as the apostle of reasonableness by signing an agreement with the Indonesian Government on the Chinese minority, and also advised his countrymen abroad to be loyal citizens of their host countries.

In terms of percentage as compared with the indigenous population, the Chinese do not constitute an impressive proportion, but when broken down the figures reveal the extent of their influence, particularly in the commercial sphere. Thus in Thailand as a whole they are only 16 per cent of the population; but in the capital, Bangkok, the nerve center of political and economic activity, they number 45 per cent. In Indonesia they are only 3 per cent, but the important cities of Jakarta and Soerabaja have a large Chinese population. This is also true of Burma, where the Overseas Chinese constitute less than 2 per cent of the population but where the Chinese section of Rangoon contains some of the most important electoral constituencies. Chinese are prominent in Manila and Cebu, but here again their over-all percentage in the Philippines is 1.5. In Singapore however they constitute 65 per cent of the population, and Malaya with Singapore accounts for 45 per cent. Every important city on the Malayan mainland is predominantly Chinese.

"If the Japanese hadn't conquered Malaya in 1942 the Chinese would have," was a remark one heard very often in Singapore soon after the last war.

Although Indians form part of the polyglot pattern of

Southeast Asia, they are neither politically, economically, nor numerically as influential as the Chinese. Even in Ceylon, where they constitute a considerable proportion of the population, the majority of them are descendants of indentured Indian laborers who were imported into the island many years ago. Malaya also contains an Indian population of around 700,000, but they are mainly laborers. In Singapore there are less than 100,000 Indians. The Indian community in Southeast Asia has been reinforced in recent years by a thin layer of businessmen with a leavening of doctors, lawyers, and teachers. But neither in numbers nor influence are the Indians comparable to the Chinese, who are as prolific as they, more sturdy, venturesome, disciplined, and purposeful.

Of all the Asian settlers in this region of lotus-eaters the Indians and Chinese are most industrious, and in almost every country of Southeast Asia both have left the stamp of their civilizations, cultures, and commerce. The Indian, however, unlike the Chinese, has never been politically expansionist. His interests have been commercial, cultural, or religious, and in the long history of India's association with this region the only rulers who have shown expansionist maritime ambitions in these waters were the Cholas who reigned from A.D. 850 to 1150. The impact which India has made on Southeast Asia has been likened by Western historians to the impact of Greece on the peoples of the Mediterranean.

Southeast Asia, containing nearly 200 million people and straddling two oceans, the Indian and the Pacific, represents the soft underbelly of Asia. A strategic area, it is peculiarly susceptible to the purposeful thrust of an aggressive Asian power, for it represents a plural polyglot society with no racial, linguistic, or religious bonds among its varied peoples. There exist, for instance, no racial affinities between the Burmese and Indonesians nor any linguistic link between the Thais and the Malays. Religiously the Buddhist Cambodians and the Catholic Filipinos are far apart. But the eyes of all of them are fixed on the two giants of Asia—India and China—whose close understanding until the Tibetan affair they viewed with uneasy suspicion.

Now that Sino-Indian relations are strained and the Chinese stand poised along India's long frontier, the countries and peoples of Southeast Asia see in India their main bulwark against the Red tide. The Chinese irredentist urge is not confined only to Bhutan, Sikkim, Nepal, and Ladakh. Over forty years ago the late Sun Yat-sen cited a long list of so-called lost territories which China would reclaim. "We lost," he declared, "Korea, Formosa, and Peng Fu to Japan after the Sino-Japanese War, Annam to France and Burma to Britain. . . . In addition the Ryukyu Islands, Siam, Borneo, Sarawak, Java, Ceylon, Nepal, and Bhutan were once tributary States to China." This is a pretty inclusive list, embracing as it does almost the whole of Southeast Asia and beyond. Chiang Kai-shek subsequently repeated these claims, and Mao Tse-tung has reiterated them. Mao in fact traces the beginnings of his political consciousness to his realization of China's territorial losses. Edgar Snow quotes him as saying, "I began to have a certain amount of political consciousness, especially after I read a pamphlet telling of the dismemberment of China . . . of Japan's occupation of Korea and Formosa, of the loss of suzerainty in Indo-China, Burma and elsewhere."

Apart from their strategic importance the countries of Southeast Asia are rich in mineral wealth and natural products. Before the last war 90 per cent of the world's rubber output came from this region, along with 60 per cent of its tin and 90 per cent of its quinine. Burma, Thailand, and Viet Nam constitute Asia's rice bowl, and though Thailand is not in actual territorial proximity with Red China, being separated from it by the northern wedge of Laos and the Shan

States, all three are in dangerous proximity to China and each is vulnerable. The Sino-Burmese frontier has not been demarcated, and Rangoon has more than once protested to Peking against territorial encroachments by Chinese troops. In 1955, a year after the declaration of Panchshila, Communist Chinese units moved into the Kla States on the plea that the boundary was vague and not defined.

Southeast Asia, though vulnerable to China, represents the "rimland" of the democratic bloc against the continental "heartland" of Communist China. This "rimland," buttressed by the vast land mass of India, is a challenge to China, a deterrent for the time being to that country which attempts to reach out to the Indian and Pacific oceans. Beyond the land curtain of Southeast Asia lie the Antipodes, a vast territorial area conspicuously underpopulated.

China's irredentist urge in these regions is concentrated in the Overseas Chinese who function as its fifth column in this area and who are the nuclei of its shock brigades. The *hua-ch'iao* serve as instruments to propagate the message of Communist China, not only politically but by commercial and cultural means. Through the Bank of China, which has branches all over Southeast Asia, the Communists bring pressure and persuasion to bear on Chinese businessmen to advance Peking's commercial policies which have basically political motivations. India and Indian businessmen have good reason to know this, for Asian economic rivalry in Southeast Asia is mainly Indo-Chinese. Since 1958 Peking has made determined efforts to undercut Indian trade and to drive Indian exporters out of Southeast Asia's markets. Chinese goods, amazingly low priced and often of high quality, have been dumped in this region, thereby stimulating the state-subsidized Chinese trade drive throughout this area. Cultural propaganda is purveyed through nearly 2,000 Chinese primary schools, over 180 middle schools, and the Nanyang

University in Singapore, and at one time this led to a small exodus of Chinese students to their homeland, only to bring back the majority of them disillusioned. But pride in the "achievements" of Communist China is still a big selling point, and appeals to the Chinese as Chinese, irrespective of their beliefs. Another medium for cultural as well as economic and political propaganda is the Chinese Overseas press. There are some seventy-five daily Chinese-language newspapers published in Southeast Asia in addition to scores of journals, and an output of motion pictures. Many of them help in propagating the Communist cult. With Peking and Taiwan two Chinas exist. But in reality there are three, for the 14 million Overseas Chinese are not negligible, and the vast majority have their eyes focused on Peking.

China's occupation of Tibet, by bringing the Communist menace to the doors of India, thus threatens the whole of Asia and the democratic world. Happily, as in India, the Chinese Communist aggression has created a revulsion of feeling against China and Communism not only in Asia but in the Middle East. Asian feeling was reflected in the sharp comments of the press and of public leaders in countries ranging from Burma to Indonesia, Ceylon to Japan, Malaya to Cambodia. "Here," wrote the Singapore *Straits Times,* "is colonialism blood-stained and rampant. Asia must condemn it."

Asia did. Until the Hungarian tragedy of 1956 Asia had identified imperialism solely with the domination and exploitation of the black, brown, and yellow races by the white, and also with the belief that Western capitalism, with its urge for cheap labor and raw materials and its hunger for new markets, incited colonialism. Hungary stirred some faint doubts. Was Communism equally capable of imperialist ruthlessness? It is true that Soviet Russia even before this had brought the countries of East Europe under her heel, but in the confused aftermath of the last war this seemed in Asian eyes the normal projection of a European war fought for power. Neither Britain nor France, Asia noted, had shed its imperial domination even after a war fought for freedom and democracy. Tibet registered another important fact, for Communist China's aggression proved that imperialism was not necessarily a European monopoly but could extend to an Asian Power capable of exercising it against a weaker Asian country. True, Japan had ravaged China before the war; but, more than China, Tibet high-lighted an imperialism at once Asian and Communist. Japan had run amok with militarists at her helm. But Chou En-lai had pledged China to Panchshila and peace.

Peking's oppression and tyranny in Tibet were an eye-opener to Asia, particularly to India. This was unashamed *Machtpolitik*. To flout Panchshila was bad enough, but to pervert it as China did by claiming that India's protest was "interference in China's internal affairs" and therefore contrary to the five principles seemed brazen and cynical effrontery. "In Tibet," wrote Jayaprakash Narayan, "we see at this moment the workings of a new imperialism, which is far more dangerous than the old because it marches under the banner of so-called revolutionary ideology."

Tibet unmasked China as a wolf in sheep's clothing. Until the Tibetan tragedy Asia had assumed that the freedom and neutrality of the newly independent nations were threatened more by the old colonial imperialists of the West buttressed by a bitterly anti-Communist America than by Russia and China, both of whom preached peaceful coexistence. Suez had deepened Asia's suspicion that the old imperialism was only dormant, not dead. But Tibet provoked a radical change in outlook. It appeared to Asia that Communist imperialism was even worse than the Western imperialism it had known and suffered under, for Communist imperialists had hitherto posed as the liberators of downtrodden countries and individuals. In Tibet, China proved that Communism was not only out to crush capitalism but that it was also equally willing to mow down the peasants and workers of any country which tried to throw off its tyrannical yoke.

It proved another thing. Asia had drawn a distinction only between the old Western imperialists and the new Communists, but as between Soviet Russia and Communist China it had also naïvely believed that while Russia could in certain circumstances be ruthless China somehow was "different." China was Asian and, like other Asian countries, had once been oppressed by the West. Now China showed itself capable of being equally ruthless against a weak and helpless Asian country.

Asia's credulity had its counterpart in the Middle East where over a long period President Nasser of Egypt had been inclined to woo the Russians. Their intervention during the Suez crisis further fortified the link. But Moscow soon showed in Iraq and elsewhere that Russia's professed friendship for the Arab world was by no means disinterested and that its clasp of friendship only too often signified the clutch of death. What both Russia and China sought to do by protestations of peace and professions of friendship was to lull the neutral independent countries into dreamy unawareness and thereby to foster the growth of Communist influence in those states which would ultimately wake up to find that they had lost both their neutrality and their independence. Moscow has demonstrated in the Arab world as China has in Tibet what exactly the Communists mean by peaceful coexistence, noninterference, and respect for territorial integrity.

The onus and responsibility for preventing further Communist infiltration into Asia now rest largely on India. Despite New Delhi's efforts to maintain friendly relations with

China while expressing deep sympathy for and continued belief in at least the regional autonomy of Tibet, it is becoming increasingly obvious that a firmer attitude and more positive action are called for if the main objective of this policy—the preservation of the security and integrity of India —is to be ensured. New Delhi's conciliatory gestures have induced no reciprocal manifestations in Peking. On the contrary Communist China's attitude has hardened, is hardening, and is likely to harden further. The harassment of Indian traders in Tibet continues, and despite India's protests, which have been ignored, the Chinese appear to have launched on a policy of systematic persecution.

During the uprising the Chinese authorities placed various obstacles in the way of persons of Indian origin, residing in Tibet, who wished to register themselves as Indian citizens at the Indian Consulate General in Lhasa. Three Indians were held in custody by the Chinese for not having travel papers or documents of nationality, although the Indian Government pointed out that these persons had gone to Tibet at a time when there was no obligation to take out such papers.

According to the Government of India there are 97 registered Indian traders in Yatung, Phari, and Gyantse and about 21,000 seasonal traders in western Tibet. No precise statistics are available about the number of Kashmiri Moslems and Ladakhi lamas, but as far as can be ascertained there are 124 families of Kashmiri Moslems with a total number of 583 individuals residing in the Lhasa-Shigatse area, while the number of lama students from Ladakh studying in various Tibetan monasteries was about 400 before the uprising. Of the latter, around 40 were among the refugees who came to India. A few of the Kashmiri Moslems are descendants of the prisoners captured by the Tibetans when a Dogra force of 5,000 men led by Zorawar Singh unsuccessfully attacked western Tibet in 1841.

Prior to 1954, when the Sino-Indian agreement on trade with Tibet was signed, travel between Ladakh and Tibet was practically free, and traditionally hundreds of Ladakhi Buddhists visited Tibet every year for religious purposes, many of them staying on as students in the monasteries. Similarly, Moslem traders came in large numbers from the same area. Very few of these traders and students had troubled to register as Indian nationals because the Chinese authorities had not been insistent on documents of nationality. There has been no response from Peking so far * to the Indian Government's plea that persons of Indian origin in Tibet who considered themselves Indian nationals should be allowed, if they so wished, to seek the advice and protection of the Indian Consul General in Lhasa or, alternatively, should be permitted to return to India.

More perturbing than these harassments is the reported concentration of large Chinese forces on Nepal's northern border and all along the Indo-Tibetan border. Disclosing this early in August, the Nepalese prime minister, B. P. Koirala, announced that his government planned to spend an additional Rs. 15 lakhs ($300,000) on defense this year. The defense of Nepal's southern border is very largely India's responsibility. Koirala also referred to "adequate measures" taken by the Nepalese Government against the infiltration of Communist agents in the northern districts and to their reported efforts for "the amalgamation of certain parts of Nepal with Tibet." Earlier reports had spoken of "the suspicious and subversive activities of some Tibetans who are perhaps Peking's agents" in the Solo Khumbu area.

Since 1856 when the Gurkhas of Nepal, having defeated the Tibetans in battle, imposed a treaty on them, Nepal has regarded Tibet as a tributary. The Manchus at that time were in no position to help the Tibetans, who were badly beaten. Under the treaty Tibet was required to pay Nepal an annual

* This is being written in August, 1959.

tribute of Rs. 10,000 ($2,000) and grant extraterritorial rights to the Nepalese in Tibet which gave them the privilege of being tried in their own country for any offense committed in Tibet and which also exempted them from trade duties. Nepal continued to receive the tribute and enjoy these extraterritorial rights until some time after the Chinese Communists overran Tibet in 1950. In a recent reference to this treaty the Nepalese prime minister remarked that "Tibet was almost under Nepal's suzerainty and paid Nepal a fixed amount for its defense. This position has changed after the occupation of Tibet by the Chinese." Incidentally Nepal itself, after being defeated by the Chinese in 1792, was required to send a quinquennial tribute to Peking which Katmandu discontinued in 1908.

Not surprisingly, relations between Nepal and Tibet have never been too cordial, though the Chinese Communists, as we noted, by favoring the Nepalese traders in Tibet as against their Indian counterparts have tried to play off the one against the other. During the period of British rule in India, Nepal, though friendly with Britain, tried to preserve her own independence by playing off China against Britain, and at times helped China to be strong in Tibet. Thus in 1909, when General Chao Ehr-feng was advancing into Tibet, Katmandu advised Lhasa not to resist. Nor, though under the 1856 treaty with Tibet the Nepalese undertook "to afford help and protection" to Tibet "as far as they can, if any foreign country attacks it," did Nepal go to Tibet's assistance when a British military expedition marched into the Chumbi Valley in 1888 or when the Younghusband expedition entered Lhasa in 1904.

It would therefore not be surprising if the first Communist probe from Tibet were directed at Nepal, which has also a considerable pro-Communist element, headed by Dr. K. I. Singh, who about eight years ago, when the Communist party was outlawed in Nepal, took refuge in Tibet. Singh has since returned to Nepal and is now a member of its legislature. China should find it to her advantage to exploit Tibetan antipathy to the Gurkhas by persuading the Tibetans to infiltrate politically into Nepal as a prelude to its absorption. Nepal is thus threatened by potential fifth columns inside and outside her borders. The mountain ranges to the north, which contain some of the highest peaks of the Himalayas, including Everest and Kinchinjunga, were at one time thought to be an impenetrable barrier. But a range of mountains no more than a barbed-wire fence can keep out ideas. The Ranas, or feudal ruling class, were overthrown in Nepal in January, 1951, and their counterparts in Tibet are on their way out. Of all the regions strung along the Indo-Tibetan border, Nepal would seem to be the most vulnerable, though Bhutan and Sikkim may also fall easy prey to Chinese infiltration.

Shortly after Communist China's first aggression on Tibet in 1950, the Indian prime minister declared that any transgression of the Indo-Tibetan border would be resisted by India and that the same principle would apply to the Nepalese-Tibetan border. India declared her determination to do this by guaranteeing the integrity of the Himalayan border states of Nepal, Sikkim, and Bhutan. Nepal's northern frontier which faces Tibet occupies, as we saw, some five hundred miles. To the east lies Sikkim, a former tributary of Tibet, with the Kumaon district of India's Uttar Pradesh on the west separated from Nepal by the Kali River. The southern border, whose defense, according to Nepal's prime minister, is largely India's responsibility, adjoins a part of Bengal and Uttar Pradesh.

From the ethnographic standpoint Sikkim, Bhutan, and Ladakh are Tibetan, which would make the area of ethnographic Tibet around 800,000 square miles with a population of about five million, the majority living in the area between Lhasa and the Chinese border. Three-fourths of Sikkim's inhabitants are Indians of Nepalese origin, but its ruler and leading personages are Tibetan, and Sikkim was originally under Tibetan rule. It is a curious fact that while along the northern border of Nepal westward to Ladakh there are many Tibetan settlements on the Indian side, no Indian settlements exist on the Tibetan side. Bound to Tibet by ties of race and religion, Sikkim, Bhutan, and Ladakh are therefore highly susceptible to propaganda from across the border.

Even in the days of British rule in India more than one Chinese spokesman urged the blending of the "five colors," these being China, Tibet, Nepal, Sikkim, and Bhutan. By bringing the three Himalayan border states under their influence, the British reared an effective barrier against Chinese infiltration, and this barrier was consolidated by the buffer of autonomous Tibet, which with its lofty altitude and large size constituted an ideal protective screen. British policy was designed to prevent military infiltration, but independent India finds itself faced with a dual threat—the threat of military infiltration and, more insidious, of political infiltration.

In the three Himalayan states which, unlike Tibet, are on the Indian side of the Himalayas, the Indian Government has taken over the policy of the British raj. No longer, however, do the Himalayan ranges and the lofty uplands of Tibet provide an effective barrier, while the MacMahon Line which defines the frontier east of Bhutan up to the intersection of the Chinese, Tibetan, and Burmese borders has never been officially recognized by China, though Nehru in reply to questions in the Lok Sabha on August 13, 1959, said that Chou En-lai had given him the definite impression some years back * that, "having regard to all the circumstances, they accepted the MacMahon Line as the international fron-

* Presumably either in 1954 when Nehru visited China or in 1956 when Chou En-lai visited India.

tier." This, like Chou's other assurances, was probably designed to lull India without completely committing China.

Recent reports tell of a mass meeting in Lhasa when the cry for the "liberation" of Ladakh, Sikkim, and Bhutan was raised by the Chinese. As on the Nepalese frontier, the Chinese are said to be massing troops on the borders of Sikkim and Bhutan. Questions were asked in the Lok Sabha in mid-August; but Nehru, while reiterating that India's territorial integrity would be "safeguarded at all costs," observed that he did not think that any large forces were concentrated on India's frontiers, although there were "very large Chinese forces all over Tibet" in the wake of the Tibetan rebellion. No doubt, said the prime minister, there were some Chinese forces on "our frontier," but India was "quite awake and alert over the matter." Replying to a query as to whether it was a fact that "as many as twenty divisions of Chinese troops are stationed in Tibet at present," Nehru remarked that he could not say—"I do not know exactly."

The questions asked in the Lok Sabha were sparked by a dispatch appearing in the London *Daily Telegraph* from its Kalimpong correspondent, quoting a speech made by the Chinese commander in Lhasa, General Chang Kuo-hua, wherein the general had declared that "the Bhutanese, Sik-kimese, and Ladakhis form a united family in Tibet. They have been subjects of Tibet and the great motherland of China and must, once again, be united and taught the Communist doctrine." In his reply Nehru said that he had read the report of the speech which had appeared in "the official Chinese newspaper" but that the particular passage mentioned was not there. "That, of course," he commented, "does not lead us to believe that it is not possible, but it is not there. . . . Anyhow, he would be an exceedingly foolish person who would make the remarks attributed to this gentleman."

Despite the assurances which India's prime minister said

he had been given on the MacMahon Line by the Chinese prime minister, which Peking was later officially to deny, thereby impliedly branding the Indian prime minister as a liar, Nehru disclosed that "discussions had taken place about some pockets along the MacMahon Line which, no doubt, would be continued." He did not specify where the disputed pockets lay. The MacMahon Line, which was defined in the Simla Convention of 1914, is concerned with securing India's northeast frontier running some eight hundred miles east of Bhutan along the northern and eastern borders of Assam to the meeting place of China, Tibet, and the Burmese hinterland. Since this frontier is around a hundred miles from the plains of India, with difficult hills and valleys between, it forms a useful barrier. Bhutan is contiguous for a little under 250 miles with the Tibetan frontier, while the boundary between Tibet and Sikkim is the crest of the mountain range separating the waters flowing into the Tista River and its affluents in Sikkim from the Machu River in Tibet and northward into other Tibetan rivers. The NEFA's northern frontier is defined by the MacMahon Line. At one point, near the 95th meridian, the line is broken by the Brahmaputra River, and although it traverses difficult terrain it has been fully surveyed except for a strip of about one hundred miles west of the Brahmaputra defile. Possibly the disputed pockets to which Nehru referred lie in this region, but the Chinese can conveniently ignore the MacMahon Line when it suits them, since the Simla Convention, in which it was incorporated, was not ratified by China. Nehru, however, has left China in no doubt that so far as India is concerned the MacMahon Line is the country's "firm, northern frontier —firm by treaty, firm by usage and firm by geography."

Ladakh, which the Chinese also claim as their natural sphere, is in northeast Kashmir, belonging to the broad valley of the upper Indus which flows from West Tibet, and is bounded to the east by the Tibetan districts of Nagri and Rudok. It contains a considerable Moslem population, descendants of the invaders from neighboring Baltistan who ravaged Ladakh in the seventeenth century. Almost all the Ladakhi traders in Tibet are Moslems, but there is also an influential community of Buddhists owing religious allegiance to the Dalai Lama. The Ladakhis, by nature quiescent, are no soldiers. This region formed part of the Tibetan Empire until its disruption in the tenth century, but its religious ties continued with Lhasa until disrupted by the Communist Chinese invasion. Now it looks as if Peking would like to revive these links under its own auspices and for its own particular purposes.

It is no longer possible to conceal (even if some in New Delhi might wish to do so) the grave deterioration in Sino-Indian relations with the turn of events in Tibet. In its long history Tibet has known many reverses and humiliations at the hands of China, but it has also had its eras and spells of good fortune, the last being when the Manchus were toppled from their throne in 1911 and Tibet knew and enjoyed nearly a half-century of freedom. As China's captive, Tibet, with its long experience of Chinese ways and means, realizes that its future role is to serve as a decoy in order to make its smaller Buddhist neighbors also captive.

Communist China will not risk a world conflagration by launching a frontal attack on India's two-thousand-mile frontier, for the ways of Communism are more insidious and calculated. What is likely to happen is a general "softening up" of the Himalayan states at India's front door as a prelude to infiltration within the inner citadel, while simultaneously the same tactics are employed elsewhere, as they have been in Burma and more recently in Laos. The Communists invariably nibble at the flanks. Inside China the national minorities will be used as baits to lure the other minorities across the border into Peking's vast and widening maw. Outside, in the sprawling regions of Southeast Asia, the fifth columns of the Overseas Chinese will be deployed. Behind the Laotian imbroglio is the long arm of Communist China.

The Indian Government, while it has given asylum to the Dalai Lama and to some twelve thousand Tibetan refugees, has repudiated the Dalai Lama's claim to regard himself and his ministers as the Government of Tibet. But the Dalai Lama, if he is an embarrassment to New Delhi inside India, is a menace and a nuisance to Peking as long as he remains outside China. His Holiness claims the allegiance of many thousands in the border states of Ladakh, Nepal, Bhutan, and Sikkim, as well as in parts of the Northeast Frontier Agency. He is India's best insurance and deterrent against Communist efforts to lure the peoples and rulers of the Himalayan states into the Chinese orbit. As long as the Dalai Lama remains an honored guest on Indian soil, he is the best safeguard against the witchery and wiles of Communist China in the frontier regions, as well as in the Buddhist lands of Southeast Asia. India knows only what the Communists do. The Dalai Lama knows what Communism is. He is a victim of its treachery, and as such the symbol of his followers' hopes and faith.

agonizing reappraisal

CHAPTER EIGHT

With China's aggression on Tibet the scales have fallen from Asia's eyes, and Asia, more particularly India, is now in the process of agonizing reappraisal.

Whether the countries of Southeast Asia succumb finally to Communist blandishments and threats depends largely on the attitude India immediately adopts. The Tibetan tragedy has high-lighted as nothing else has done the inherent contradictions in India's foreign policy. On principle India's policy is the right policy for India and for the newly independent countries of Asia, provided neutrality or nonalignment is positive and not "on one side." India cannot consistently condemn Communist China for her oppression in Tibet and sponsor her membership for the United Nations. If nothing else, Tibet has proved that the distinction between the aggressor and the victim is no more academic than the distinction between Communist and democratic beliefs. India was rightly vigorous in her condemnation of the Anglo-French aggression on Egypt in October, 1956, but it is difficult to defend her lukewarm attitude to the brutalities perpetrated in Hungary by Soviet Russia about the same time. If Indian condemnation of the Western action in Suez was justified, as it undoubtedly was, and did not lead to any intensification of the hot war, why make the excuse that India's restrained criticism of China's action on Tibet was inspired by a desire to do nothing to aggravate an inflammable situation? It is unconvincing. As a result of her attitude to Suez, India did not lose the friendship of Britain and France, but she seems to have lost the good will of Communist China by her mild criticism of its government's action in Tibet. Nothing could demonstrate more clearly the difference between what the democratic and Communist worlds understand by friendship. To the Communists friendship plainly is friendship on their own terms.

The revulsion which Russia's brutal suppression of the Hungarian uprising provoked in Europe is paralleled in Asia by China's crushing of the Tibetan rebellion. Asia has suddenly discovered that the Chinese Communists are not different from the Soviet Communists and that the objectives and methods of Communist imperialism, whether Russian or Chinese, are the same. Communism is by nature expansionist, for its aim is to transform and rule the world.

Tibet has highlighted the menace posed by this fact, and dramatically if also tragically revealed the cynicism and cruelty of Communism. Less than a year after the Budapest rising, Khrushchev was impudently asserting that Hungary was "an independent State with its own independent Government," * while Chou En-lai in the eight years preceding the Chinese absorption of Tibet had blandly assured Nehru more than once that Peking meant to respect Tibetan autonomy. While Russia was the strongest power in Europe, China emerged after Japan's defeat in the Second World War as the major military state in Asia, determined to assert her right to Central Asia and to be that continent's leading

* In an interview given to the *New York Times*, May 10, 1957.

Power. In the former plan her ambitions lay, ironically enough, across the path of Russia, for in north and northwest China are the frontier regions of Manchuria, Mongolia, and Sinkiang, whose peoples are akin to those across the border in Soviet Russia. One reason why Peking, unlike Moscow, has not given its so-called autonomous regions the theoretical right of secession may possibly be because of China's lurking fear that these frontier regions might cast their lot with their neighbors across the border. To believe that there are not internal rivalries within the camp of international Communism is to misread its character.

Basically, however, the impulses which motivate Communist states are similar, for Communism grows by what it feeds on and its intrinsic expansionist urge is impelled by the necessity to clear obstacles in its path inside and outside its boundaries. An autonomous region such as Tibet, Inner Mongolia, Sinkiang, Ningsia, or Chinghai was an obstacle not only to the fulfillment of the Communist program in its own area but to some extent in China itself. Opposition in Tibet combined with the Dalai Lama's threat to remain in India in 1956 induced Peking the following year to call a temporary halt to its "democratic reforms" in Tibet. Similarly the Chinese encountered resistance to their efforts at ideological infiltration in Chinghai, which borders Tibet and which has a population consisting largely of national minorities such as the Moslem Dungans and the Tibetan Buddhists who acknowledge the spiritual authority of the Dalai Lama. It became necessary for the Chinese Communists to sweep aside both these obstacles. The same pattern repeats itself in Europe. West Germany is an obstacle to the fulfillment of the Soviet plan not only in East Germany but in Eastern Europe and therefore requires to be swept away. Hence the Russian description of West Berlin as "a cancerous growth."

What the Tibetan tragedy has done is to expose the real character of Communism to Asia and to impress on it the fact that Communism changes its mask but never its character, whether such Communism masquerades as Asian or European. Those in its dangerous propinquity see the point when the menace actually threatens them as India has belatedly done, and also the United Arab Republic. A Cairo pamphlet issued by the Information Department of the U.A.R. Government shortly after China's aggression in Tibet described Peking's action as "imperialistic," and linked Tibet with Iraq as part of a grand plan by international Communism to "subvert positive neutrality and nonalignment." It is an interesting comment since its implication is that what the Communists expect from the neutral nations is to be "neutral on one side." The logical conclusion which follows from this is that Panchshila means peaceful coexistence on Communist terms and as the Reds understand and interpret it. These are the facts to which non-Communist Asia has at last awakened.

It has been hinted in New Delhi that the facts of history must be recognized and that Tibet having been under Chinese domination off and on, the question of her independence cannot be raised at this stage. Hungary, for one, was long under the domination of the Austro-Hungarian Empire and is now, despite Khrushchev's assertion, under the heel of Soviet Russia. Does that mean that Hungary is thereby condemned to perpetual subjugation? The Chinese Communists, it is also hinted, are converting Tibet from a feudal into a progressive state, an argument often advanced by British apologists for British rule in India, and rightly condemned at the time by Indian nationalists, including Nehru. How can India square her justification of the fact of China's imposition of "progress" on Tibet with her condemnation of the same process by the British in India?

Tibet should induce not only second thoughts but clearer

thinking. The hard-won freedom of the newly independent countries of Asia is no longer threatened by the old colonialism of the West but by the new imperialism of the Communist bloc which must burst its boundaries or be broken. Expansionism is endemic to the Communist system. "We Communists and revolutionary cadres," declared a Chinese monthly,* "should not merely know the world but, what is more important, transform the world." The Communism of Stalin, Khrushchev and Mao Tse-tung is far removed and different from the Communism preached by Karl Marx, who propounded it as a scientific study of society. Though Nehru has stated that he dislikes dogmatism and the treatment of Karl Marx's writings or any other books as "revealed scripture which cannot be challenged," and has also expressed his detestation of regimentation and heresy hunts, it would seem from his attitude toward Soviet Russia and Communist China that what he objects to in them is primarily their too easy resort to violence. He did not, for instance, object in 1950 to China's claim to assert its "sovereignty or, if you like, suzerainty" in Tibet but only asked Peking to do it "peacefully." This was tantamount to asking a tiger to deal with a lamb mercifully.

By her aggression on Tibet, China is revealed as a cruel imperialist Power with the old Han spirit of expansionism intensified by the new spirit of Communist colonialism. Had Communism, as Jayaprakash Narayan pointed out, been a truly liberating and anti-imperialist force, the Chinese Communists on assuming power would themselves have shed voluntarily the old imperialist notion of suzerainty and entered into a treaty with Tibet of equality and friendship. This would have been in line with what the early Bolsheviks did on assuming power in Russia and with what Lenin laid down when the Soviet took over the government of the coun-

* *Hsuch Hsi* (Political Study), monthly Peking periodical No. 5, 1955.

try. "If," declared Lenin,* "any nation whatsoever is de-
tained by force within the boundaries of a certain State, and
if that nation contrary to its expressed desire—whether such
desire is made manifest in the Press, National Assembly,
Party decisions, or in protests and uprisings against national
oppression—is not given the right to determine the form of
its state of life by free voting, and completely free from the
presence of troops of the annexing or stronger State and without the least pressure, then the adjoining of that nation by
the stronger State is annexation, i.e., seizure by force and
violence."

India's mistake, as we saw, was twofold. Presented with an
opportunity to treat Tibet as independent, New Delhi chose
to accept the Chinese claim to suzerainty on the plea that this
concept was a British legacy left in the lap of independent
India which India could not repudiate, even while New Delhi
repudiated other imperialist legacies in Tibet, such as the
privilege of stationing small Indian military units at Yatung
and Gyantse. The second mistake which India made, and
under which the Indian Government still seems to labor,
was to trust explicitly and implicitly every assurance given
to it by the Chinese Communists even when experience had
proved how utterly untrustworthy were the pledges and
promises freely made by Peking. History might find it hard to
exonerate India of the charge that consciously or unconsciously she aided and abetted Peking on obliterating and
absorbing Tibet. If she did it consciously, a theory which
this writer does not accept, it was undoubtedly a crime. If
India did it unconsciously, as the records suggest, it was
folly. The celebrated words of Fouché on the murder of the
Duc d'Enghien are apposite in this context: "It was worse
than a crime. It was a blunder."

* In "Decree on Peace" (1917), quoted in *Works* (4th Russian edition),
Vol. 26, p. 218.

There is an interesting parallel in the development of Communism and capitalism to which many Asian intellectuals, notably Jayaprakash Narayan, have drawn insistent attention. Nineteenth century capitalism under the leadership of Britain, France, and Germany became progressively aggressive and expansionist, acquiring in time in Asian and African eyes the stamp of colonialism. So also now, the Communism of Marx, which once stood for the freedom of the proletariat and the oppressed peoples of the world, who were invited to throw off the chains and shackles which bound them, has emerged as an imperialism which threatens the liberty of both. As Jayaprakash Narayan again has observed: "Somewhere or the other Marxism had gone wrong. Lenin wrote a famous thesis on imperialism as the last phase of capitalism. Someone should write another thesis on Communism as the first phase of a new imperialism." In short, Communism, in its contemporary form, whether Asian or European has revealed itself for what it really is—not a progressive force identified with humanism, equality, and freedom, but a medieval tyranny threatening the liberty of millions of unoffending peoples, members largely of the weaker nations of the world.

Nehru's moderation in condemning the new Communist imperialism, as compared with his unequivocal attacks on the old colonialism of the West, puzzles and confuses not only India but also Asia and Africa, which still lay great store—and rightly—by his utterances. Until quite recently Nehru was inclined to view Marxism through the rose-tinted spectacles of the early 1930's when as a member of the Communist-sponsored League Against Imperialism he saw Communism not as another form of totalitarianism which threatened democracy, but as a shield protecting the weaker colonial countries against the unceasing rapacity of the imperialist Powers masquerading behind the mask of democracy. As matters have developed in Tibet, the choice before India is plain. As long as it was possible to press for the recognition of Tibetan autonomy, while maintaining friendly relations with Communist China in order to ensure the major aim of Indian policy, which is the security and integrity of India itself, what the veteran Chakravarti Rajagopalachari * described as New Delhi's "tightrope-walking line" was justified. But once it was clear that the two could not be simultaneously pursued, one of them had to be dropped. Nehru's mistake lay in continuing to maintain both, even when confronted by mounting obloquy from China. The contrast in Peking's reactions to New Delhi's protests over China's aggression on Tibet in 1950 and again in 1959 is striking and significant.

In 1950, after first sharply rebuffing India and asking it to mind its own business, Peking found it wise to assume a pose of reasonableness, and in the Sino-Tibetan treaty of May, 1951, agreed to respect Tibetan autonomy and the position of the Dalai Lama as the supreme spiritual and temporal ruler of Tibet in return for Lhasa's recognition of Chinese suzerainty and of Peking's authority over its external affairs. Peking, of course, had no intention of keeping these promises; but at that time, with the Korean War on her hands, Communist China was in no position further to exacerbate world opinion and intensify Asian uneasiness. At this juncture India was the monkey that the Chinese tiger utilized for pulling Peking's chestnuts out of the fire.

In the following years China's strategy was to lull and mollify opinion abroad, particularly in Asia, while trying to stifle Tibet's regional autonomy behind the screen of the bamboo curtain. Hence her pose as the defender of Asian interests, the champion of the war against colonialism, and the

* Former Governor General of India and now leader of the newly formed Swantantra party in opposition to the Congress party.

protector of the freedom of the newly independent countries of Asia. With the same purpose in view Peking subscribed to Panchshila in the preamble of the Sino-Indian treaty on Tibet in April, 1954, reaffirmed it in the Sino-Indian statement of June, 1954, and at Bandung in the following year reiterated its belief in the Five Principles while protesting its "peaceful intentions" toward the small nations of Asia.

Simultaneously inside Tibet the Chinese Communists were trying in every way to browbeat and batter that country into subjection. As the Dalai Lama observed in an interview to a Burmese newspaper editor in August, 1959: "The cruel attempt to wipe out the Tibetan race has not just come about. It is a long-range program which was first introduced in 1949–50." * Not long after the Chinese forces had entered Lhasa, the Tibetans, as we saw, grew restive and by the end of 1951, on the testimony of General Chang Kuo-hua, they were beginning to organize resistance. In the Dalai Lama's words, the Communists at first tried "subversion without open violence. Their earliest primary schools taught the Tibetan language as well as Tibetan prayers. But gradually the Tibetan prayers were dropped and then the Tibetan language gave way to Chinese." Yet, as we have seen, the tempo of Tibetan resistance grew and in time erupted into open rebellion, compelling the Communists in 1957 temporarily to retrace their steps.

In April, 1958, Peking set up its rural communes inside China proper in the central province of Honan, and by December, 1958, the Communists claimed to have established a total of 26,000 communes covering 99 per cent of China's peasant households, that is, 120 million households. Before the spring of 1959, when it was planned that the communes would be fully operational, opposition to this policy of

* Presumably when the Communists had established their regime in Peking.

"regimentation of the people" had crystallized both in China proper and in the minority regions where the communes had almost simultaneously been imposed. On October 9, 1958, the Peking *People's Daily* castigated the critics and skeptics, adding that the ideologies of individualism, parochialism, and capitalism could still cause mischief, and urging that "the struggle" be continued. Two days previously the same paper had ominously recommended that a "little rectification campaign" should be launched. Early in 1959 party cadres were summoned from Tibet to China to study the working of the new communes, and the Dalai Lama himself had been invited to Peking in April. Internal exigencies and external pressures thus compelled Communist China to drop its mask. This it finally did when the revolt of the Khamba tribesmen in western Szechwan infected Tibet, threatening Lhasa itself. The mailed fist replaced the not so velvet glove.

Peaceful coexistence served the countries of Asia as long as Peking was prepared to respect the principles of Panchshila. China's naked aggression on Tibet had shocked not only the smaller Asian countries such as Burma and Cambodia, but also India, into the realization that unless they confront the new imperialism more resolutely the same fate awaits them. This is the great lesson which Tibet has taught. In retrospect it was foolish and complacent for India to have taken Communist China's assurances at their face value and to have believed that a powerful totalitarian state could be trusted to respect a small country's autonomy which it had pledged itself to honor. India, however, is not the only victim of Communist guile.

Nehru's statements in the Lok Sabha on August 13th suggest that the Indian Government has at long last awakened to the threat which Communist imperialism poses to Asia. Some faint stirring of doubt was already evident in an earlier statement Nehru had made in the course of a speech in

August, 1958, explaining to his party the difference between Communism and Indian Socialism. "It [Communism] is failing," he observed, "because of its rigidity, because suppression of individual liberty is bringing about powerful reactions, because of its contempt for the moral and spiritual side of life, and because it tends to deprive human behavior of standards of values." Owing to these deficiencies, Nehru prophesied that Communism "eventually will be overthrown." As was to be expected, neither the analysis nor the prophecy was received kindly by Moscow or Peking. Yet even to many democrats Nehru's prophecy that the Communist system would eventually be overthrown because of the intrinsic evil it enshrines would seem to presuppose that only the good flourish on earth—which as a presumption is glib and dangerously near wishful thinking.

Peking has not only denied Nehru's statement that Chou En-lai had repeatedly assured him that China accepted the MacMahon Line but it has also claimed an area of 90,000 kilometers on the Indian side of the Himalayas which would include the entire NEFA area and more, and bring the Chinese to the north bank of the Brahmaputra River. As Nehru said in the Lok Sabha, it amounted to a claim by the Chinese for "the Himalayas being handed over as a gift to them," and added, "It is the pride and arrogance that is showing in their language, in their behavior to us, and in so many things that they have done."

Characteristically, having repudiated his previous assurance on the MacMahon Line, the Chinese prime minister now assures India that Sikkim and Bhutan do not enter into the present Sino-Indian dispute. Nehru, a wiser and sadder man, in announcing this to Parliament reiterated the Indian Government's pledge to protect the borders of those states, interference with which would be the same as interference with the borders of India. At the moment of writing, the Chinese are still in possession of the Indian checkpost of Longju, ten miles inside the Indian border, and have declined to accept New Delhi's suggestion that they withdraw as a preliminary to negotiations on disputed points in the MacMahon Line.

Communism cannot be wished out of existence any more than it can be wished out of international life. Some more purposeful and positive attitude and action are needed if Asia is first to counter and then to conquer this menace. Nehru has often emphasized and is himself sincere in declaring that India's foreign policy is not motivated by fear, but there is no denying that the attitude of the general Indian public toward Communist China is a mixture of admiration and fear, and in turn provokes from the Chinese a mixture of threats and blandishments. Some foreign observers see in the passionate attachment of India, Burma, Indonesia, and Cambodia to the principles of coexistence an admission by these countries of their belief that these principles provide the only guarantee against aggression by China. The alternative is war, which they are not prepared to face. But this alternative is precisely what they must realistically face and be prepared for. On the surface China's attitude toward India is one of condescending friendship, described starkly by a recent Indian visitor to that country, Dr. Chandrasekhar, as an attitude ranging from "total ignorance to absolute contempt."

In 1948, a year before the Communists officially assumed the government of China, the so-called Southeast Asian Youth Conference, a Communist front, which met in Calcutta, adopted the Zhdanov line decreeing violent revolution against the governments of the newly independent countries of Asia, including India, Burma, Indonesia, and other areas such as Malaya and Indonesia. Although India had been among the countries which very early decided to recognize

Red China, the Communist Chinese had no hesitation in denouncing the members of the Indian Government as "bourgeois reactionaries," "lackeys," "stooges of capitalism," and "running dogs of Anglo-American imperialism." India was labeled in the Peking press as "an Anglo-American gendarme in the East." Even when another change of front was later decreed by international Communism, China's attitude toward India remained one of suspended judgment. When the nonaligned countries of Asia, headed by India, pressed for Communist China's admission to the United Nations, and refused to declare China an aggressor in Korea and to put an embargo on war materials to China, Peking displayed no great gush of gratitude. It blew hot and cold according to what its own interests demanded.

The primary aim of New Delhi's policy being to ensure the country's security and integrity, anything which endangers either cannot but be resisted. This also Nehru has latterly emphasized. On his first visit to the United States in 1949, while addressing the House of Representatives, the Indian prime minister declared: "Where freedom is menaced, or justice threatened, or where aggression takes place, we cannot be and shall not be neutral." He had earlier expressed the same sentiment in a speech he made soon after independence in March, 1948: "We are not citizens of a weak or mean country, and I think it is foolish for us to get frightened even from a military point of view, of the greatest of the Powers today. Not that I delude myself about what can happen to us if a great Power in a military sense goes against us; I have no doubt it can injure us. But after all in the past as a national movement, we opposed one of the greatest of World Powers." Joint defense measures have recently been initiated between Indian and Nepal should the latter's northern frontier be encroached upon by forces across the border in Tibet, while in NEFA the Assam Rifles have been replaced by regular military units and maintain a ceaseless vigil along the border. Within India the Union Home Ministry has alerted those responsible for detecting and preventing the percolation of subversive ideas from outside or clandestinely from inside through the Communist "grapevine" or underground. The dismissal by India's president of the Communist Government of Kerala in July, 1959, and the establishment of President's Rule in that state have irked the Reds, who had looked on Kerala as a springboard for more extensive infiltration, and regarded it as India's Yenan.

Public opinion in India had even earlier begun to assert itself more vigorously in favor of a firmer policy toward Red China. The past ten years' developments have shown that in the Communist vocabulary friendship is a unilateral business where the Communists invariably take but rarely give. India's friendly gestures have provoked, at the most, condescending acknowledgment and sometimes, as after Tibet, cold indifference and open contempt. Nothing reveals this more clearly than the language employed by the Chinese in the notes exchanged between Peking and New Delhi since 1954. In April, shortly after a procession of Indian demonstrators in Bombay had pelted a portrait of Mao Tse-tung with rotten tomatoes and eggs, the Chinese Embassy in New Delhi sent the Indian Ministry of External Affairs the following note: "Such an act of pasting the portrait of the Chairman of the People's Republic of China on the wall and throwing tomatoes and rotten eggs at it is a huge insult [which] the masses of 650 million Chinese people absolutely cannot tolerate, and it must be reasonably settled. . . . In case the reply from the Indian Government is not satisfactory the Embassy is instructed to make it clear that the Chinese Government will again raise this matter, and the Chinese side will never come to a stop, that is to say, never come to a stop even for 100 years."

Later, on May 16th, the Chinese ambassador followed up

this elegant epistle with another note: "The Chinese Government has no obligation to give assurances to any foreign country, nor can it tolerate others under the pretext of so-called different autonomy to obstruct Chinese sovereignty in Tibet. . . . Nevertheless there appeared in India before and after the rebellion in Tibet large quantities of words and deeds slandering China and interfering in China's affairs. For instance, responsible politicians and publications openly called Tibet a 'country,' and demanded that the Tibet question be submitted to the United Nations. . . .

"You can wait and see. As the Chinese proverb goes, 'The strength of the horse is borne out by the distance travelled. . . .' You will ultimately see whether the relations between the Tibet region of China and India are friendly or hostile by watching up to a hundred years. The quarrel between our two countries in the past few years and particularly in the past three months is but an interlude and does not warrant a big fuss." The note concluded: "Our Indian friends! What is your mind? Friends! It seems to us that you too cannot have two fronts. Is it not so? If it is, here, then, lies the meeting point of our two sides. Will you please think it over?"

To this India's rejoinder was polite but pointed: "It is a matter of particular surprise and disappointment that a Government and people noted for their high culture and politeness should have committed this serious lapse and should have addressed the Government of India in a language unbecoming even if it were addressed to a hostile country. Since it is addressed to a country which is referred to as friendly, this can only be considered as an act of forgetfulness."

Referring to the Bombay incident, the reply of the Indian Secretary General of External Affairs reminds the Chinese ambassador that in "India, unlike China, the law recognizes many parties and gives protection to the expression of differing opinion." It goes on to state: "That is a right guaranteed by our constitution and contrary to the practice prevailing in China. The Government of India is often criticized and opposed by sections of the Indian people. It is evident that this freedom of expression and civil liberties in India are not fully appreciated by the Government of China.

"From the statement made on behalf of the People's Government of China, it appears that the five principles of peaceful coexistence may or may not be applied according to convenience or circumstances. This is an approach with which the Government of India is not in agreement. They will continue to hold to these principles and endeavor to apply them." Peking, however, has artfully if obviously sought to differentiate between Nehru and the Indian people with the probable intention of inducing the prime minister to pay more heed to Peking's ruffled feelings than to the indignant opinions voiced by his own people. Those who know Nehru realize how vain are China's hopes and how mistaken and confused is their understanding of the relationship between India's people and their prime minister. After referring to the "large volume of slanderous utterances" which had appeared in India, an article in the Peking *People's Daily* of May 6, 1959, states: "Prime Minister Nehru is different from many persons who bear obvious ill-will toward China. He disagrees somewhat with us on the Tibetan question. But in general he advocates Sino-Indian friendship. Of this we have no doubts whatsoever." Obviously the Chinese Communists, despite their vituperative outbursts against India, lay great store by Sino-Indian "friendship," which, however strained and tenuous, they calculate on utilizing and exploiting when the occasion suits them.

The likelihood, however, is that the Chinese will not venture the risk of being involved in a global war which would almost certainly follow any armed incursion into India. Their methods of infiltration will be more subtle and subterranean. They will try to seep through Southeast Asia, not by force of arms but by the injection of subversive ideas in regions which provide the classical conditions for the reception of Communist dogmas. These regions combine illiteracy and economic underdevelopment with poverty and widespread unemployment.

Since the last war Asia has loomed large on the global horizon, and in Asia Communist China has the advantage of working in an area which Soviet Russia has "softened up" over a period of thirty years. Like the Japanese who before the last war preached "Asian co-prosperity" when they meant Japanese prosperity, the Russians had preached freedom for Asia when their design was to substitute Soviet domination for Western domination. A great many Asian countries realized this with time; but when the Communists seized power in China, Asia tended to look starry-eyed at Peking with a mixture of friendly interest, admiration, and sympathy. Later came fear and, with it, caution. In the early years of Communist rule in China, Mao Tse-tung and his henchmen categorized countries such as India, Burma, Thailand, and the Philippines as "colonial and semicolonial" lands whom the Communists should "liberate." In November, 1948, a year after India achieved independence, Liu Shao-chi, who has been elected to succeed Mao Tse-tung as Chairman of the Chinese People's Republic, in his book *Internationalism and Nationalism* called on the Communists in Asian countries to "adopt" a firm and irreconcilable policy against national betrayal by the reactionary section of the bourgeoisie, especially the big bourgeoisie which has already surrendered to imperialism. If this were not done it would be a grave mistake. Naturally when Peking talked of "liberation" it meant being "liberated" to Communism.

Though Liu's call was directed to the indigenous Reds, it was also an invitation to the fifth columns within the Overseas Chinese to overthrow their "bourgeois" regimes. In this dewey-eyed period China posed as the savior of all Asia, the Communist Moses who would lead the downtrodden peoples of Asia into the Promised Land. There were, as we saw, to be shifts and changes in this original line, but the general strategy was to remain consistent. "All Overseas Chinese," said Ho Hsiang-ming, director of Overseas Chinese Affairs in April, 1950, "should unite, support the motherland, and strengthen their unity. Strong and broad patriotic unity among all Overseas Chinese, irrespective of class, occupation, political views, or religious beliefs should be developed." Peking evidently lost no time in organizing and mobilizing its shock brigades abroad. After the developments in Tibet this process is likely to be intensified, and pressure brought to bear on those Overseas Chinese still reluctant to commit themselves to Peking.

Singapore, Malaya, and Indonesia, along with Burma, will probably be the focal points of this infiltration, though Southeast Asia as a whole, with its large Chinese communities, is generally vulnerable. Burma has been bedeviled in her relations with both Peking and Taiwan, for Kuomintang troops, retreating before the Communists, were at one time settled in fairly large numbers * in northern Burma along the Chinese and Thai borders. America's good offices have more recently been used to persuade Chiang Kai-shek to withdraw them from the country. The dispute with the Chinese Communists, on the other hand, concerns Upper Burma where a triangular northern tip of territory, comprising some 75,000 square miles, abuts on Yunnan. The greater part of this disputed line was settled by 1941, when the war interrupted the negotiations, but a considerable stretch north of 25° 35′ north

* Estimated at around 12,000.

latitude remained unsettled, and gave the Communists an opportunity to use the stratagem of shifting frontiers in a region where borders and boundaries are largely notional. In 1955, as we saw, the Communist Chinese marched their troops into the Kla States on the plea that the boundary was vaguely demarcated. This area, it has been claimed by both the Nationalists and the Communists, was part of a state which had paid tribute to China since the Tang dynasty in the seventh century. In 1947 the Nationalist Government laid claim to the northern triangle, but the Burmese Government reacted strongly. When the Communists seized power in China they neither reiterated the Nationalist claim nor renounced it, preferring to leave the position ambiguous until circumstances favored direct intrusion. The 1955 incursion is a portent of things to come, but the Burmese Government will probably be as unyielding as it was with the Nationalists in 1947. Inside Burma the Communists have been weakened by factionalism and, though offering fitful opposition to the government, constitute no immediate threat. More dangerous and insidious are the 300,000 Overseas Chinese in Burma.

In Indochina, Peking has its shock brigades in the Communist Government of North Vietnam headed by the faithful Ho Chi-minh. This Red baliwick covers approximately 62,000 square miles with its capital at Hanoi, and through it Peking seeks to stir up trouble in the southern Republic of Vietnam and in Cambodia, having already done so in Laos. Indochina, north and south, contains around one million Chinese, and its proximity to China which lowers over it to the north, makes it an easy and obvious prey.

In Thailand and Indonesia the national governments have cracked down vigorously on any infiltration move by the Chinese. Thailand maintains diplomatic relations with the Nationalists and is vigilant in its scrutiny and control of its

Chinese population, which numbers nearly three million. Adjacent to Burma, Laos, and Cambodia, it is sensitive and susceptible to pressures in this area, whether generally Chinese or specifically Communist. Thailand is not afraid of Communism. Thailand is afraid of China. Throughout Southeast Asia every regime following the Manchu dynasty has sought to expand Chinese influence, and Thailand, which tried to preserve a precarious independence between the contending rivalries of France and Britain, only to be overrun by the Japanese in the last war, does not relish the prospect of being subject to another manifestation of Chinese chauvinism which is Han Communism.

Sukarno's government once came down heavily on the Nationalist Chinese by closing their schools, newspapers, and banks and rounding up their leaders, but Indonesia, with its totalitarian tendencies, might still be more susceptible to Chinese Communist influences than most other areas in Southeast Asia. The Chinese number over two million in Indonesia and, despite Chou En-lai's much propagandized appeal to be good and loyal citizens, they know that Peking does not spurn such local citizens as potential Chinese citizens. They realize only too well that they are Peking's fifth column in Indonesia, and many of them appreciate their role and are prepared to play it.

Singapore, with its preponderating Chinese majority, as well as the Malayan mainland, whose population is 45 per cent Chinese, would appear to be more vulnerable than Indonesia to the threats and blandishments of Peking. But both these regions, having had a taste of Communist violence in the prolonged bandit insurrection, might be expected to know not only what the Communists do but what Communism is. Unfortunately, in Singapore the results of the latest elections show that Peking has found fertile soil in the contentious class conflicts which assail that island, proving one fact—that the future of the Overseas Chinese will be spelled out in local terms and measured largely by local problems, although the achievements or setbacks of the mainland Communists will undoubtedly help to tilt the scales one way or the other. Taiwan offers no practical alternative to Peking. But more and more Chinese intellectuals and businessmen in Malaya, disillusioned by the fate of their class in Communist China, are beginning to think again.

In the Overseas Chinese Peking has a weapon, at once secret and overt, which the democracies would be foolish to discount or dismiss. The Red-inclined among them can and are being used, as they will be employed in the near future, for various purposes—to incite unrest and provoke strife, to serve as the advance guards of Communist infiltration, to work as spies and contact men, to be exploited as alibis for sudden intervention. They are the Praetorian guard within the citadel and among the forces of Communist expansionism.

To counter their insidious influence will be a difficult task, for through them the Chinese Communists hope to breach the walls which ring the countries of Southeast Asia. The one sure way of countering Communist China's divisive moves is by the rapid growth of a free Southeast Asia where the Overseas Chinese, as members of a free country and community, would be assimilated in this region's multiracial polyglot fabric and by their industry, enterprise, purposefulness, and skills help in the creation of strong, independent Southeast Asian governments. A move has already been made in this direction with the establishment of self-government on the Malayan mainland and the first elections in Singapore. But it is worth noting that the government elected is pro-Communist. The Marshall Plan forced the Soviet steamroller into reverse in Europe. An Asian Marshall Plan might yet salvage that continent from Communism and stop the Chinese juggernaut in its tracks.

Is Russia as complacent as she seems over the aggressive thrust of Communist China in Asia? If India were to be converted to or coerced into Communism, Moscow would be faced by a mammoth land mass peopled, along with China, by over one-third of the world's population, and capable, despite the Atomic Age, of trading space for time and numbers for nuclear power. It is in Soviet Russia's interests that Asia should not be made Communist too quickly. Just as Peking has been wary of Russia as a potential threat to her northern and northwestern flanks in the frontier regions of Manchuria, Mongolia, and Sinkiang, so also Moscow is acutely sensitive to the threat posed by the presence of an Asian colossus which is also Communist along the exposed southeastern border of Soviet Russia. What has been described as "a muted controversy" has been proceeding for some time between Communism's two leading protagonists, and it dates back even before Khrushchev and the final ascendancy of Mao in China. Mao's tactics in the struggle against the Kuomintang deviated from orthodox Communist methodology, which had stipulated that in colonial or semicolonial countries the proletariat or urban workers must spearhead the revolution against capitalist-colonial power. China's revolution was achieved successfully by the peasantry. Peking has acknowledged itself as an ally of Moscow but never as its satellite. Stalin had presented a characteristically ambivalent front toward Mao, and shortly after Potsdam had signed a treaty with Chiang Kai-shek. Not until late in 1954, when Khrushchev and Bulganin visited China, were Sino-Russian relations made normalized. They have yet to be stabilized. Mao for a brief period in 1956 seemed to encourage the Polish Communists to break away from Mos-

cow's apron strings, while during the interlude of the "hundred flowers" Chinese suspicions of Russian designs on the
peripheral provinces of China were freely expressed. More
recently the differences came to a head with the introduction of communes into China, which Khrushchev scoffed at
as an exploded experiment in which Russia had unsuccessfully indulged. At the root of this quarrel was Moscow's
suspicion that China was "growing assertive and was too big
for its boots" and was aspiring to the political and ideological
leadership of the Communist fold. Though Moscow supported Peking in its action on Tibet, the tone of its approval
was noticeably lukewarm.

All of which demonstrates that conflict is endemic as much
within the Communist system as between the totalitarian
and democratic worlds. If Moscow in Europe and Peking in
Asia each set out to conquer new worlds, the success of each
can end only in a head-on collision between both.

Tibet's tragedy underlines many lessons for Asia and the
world, revealing at once the strength and weakness of the
Communist doctrine and system. There can be neither compromise nor coexistence with Communism. Monolithic in
its structure, it represents the resurrection of a brute force
which, believing that might is right, would return to the
laws of the jungle—trampling on the weak and the helpless,
stamping out the smallest spark of individualism, caring
nothing for personal freedom or human honor, respecting
neither the dignity of man nor the right of small countries
to live their own lives.

Tibet is dead. But if in dying it has taught a lesson that
will save Asia from the monstrous fate which befell it, Tibet,
with Asia's awakening to the real character of Communist
cruelty and tyranny, might yet be revived and live again.

with the dalai lama

(A POSTSCRIPT)

On September 8th, while in Delhi, I was able to have an interview with the Dalai Lama and to assess something of his personality, outlook, and opinions. I had seen him earlier in Mussoorie in May but had not met him or spoken to him.

His Holiness has an extremely affable and agreeable personality. He is, moreover, a perceptive and intelligent young man, well informed on certain matters and eager to know more on various topics. His manner is friendly, almost informal, and he asked me about as many questions as I asked him. What struck me most was the sense of loneliness and nostalgia which he exuded and which made his conversation in a way pathetic and touching. Had I seen much of the world, he inquired. I replied that I had seen a fair deal. Had I been to China. Yes, twice; once under Kuomintang and again under the Communists.

He spoke then of China and of Tibet. When in 1950 the Tibetans through El Salvador had taken their case against China to the United Nations, India, said His Holiness, had expressed her belief that the dispute could be settled peacefully and by negotiation. Largely on that assurance the other nations had agreed that the matter should not be discussed further and that the appeal should be withdrawn. This was done. A Sino-Tibetan agreement had subsequently been signed in 1951, only to be broken by the Chinese, who had later resorted to force. Should not India, asked His Holiness, support Tibet's latest appeal to the United Nations in the circumstances? I replied that in my opinion India certainly should, though our prime minister had already indicated his mind on the matter.

Evidently the possibility of a Sino-Soviet rift, should Moscow draw nearer to the West, weighs on Tibetan minds, for His Holiness asked my opinion on the Khrushchev-Eisenhower meeting. I answered at some length. It was a mistake to assume that there were no inner conflicts and contradictions within the Communist camp. In India only recently we had seen the spectacle of the Kerala chief minister, Mr. Namboodiripad, conditionally accepting Mr. Nehru's suggestion for midterm elections, only to be repudiated by the National Council of the Communist Party. It was my feeling, I said, that Russia was not at all anxious that India should go Communist so quickly, for otherwise Moscow, checkmated in Europe, would be faced with the great land mass of India and China backed up by their tremendous populations. It followed that if China secured the mastery of Asia, and Russia was predominant in Europe, the next head-on collision would be between the two of them.

From the Dalai Lama's animated appearance it was obvious that he was interested in that line of argument. I asked him what his own views were on it. He shrugged his shoulders, and a boyish, strangely wistful smile suddenly lit his face. "I don't know," he said with an air of helplessness. "I've never seriously thought about it." Perhaps he was reluctant to express his own view, and one could understand that.

Only on one issue, when I observed that Peking made promises only to break them, was he verbally forthright.

"That," remarked the Dalai Lama, "is the way of the Communist Chinese."

I asked him who he believed would take up Tibet's case before the United Nations. He replied somewhat somberly that he did not know, but implied, though he did not directly say so, that he was consulting "some of the smaller nations." Whether he had in mind his legal consultations with Norway's Trygve Lie, who had declined the brief, or whether he had in view some of the smaller Afro-Asian countries it was difficult to decipher, and obviously unfair to press and pursue.

Would His Holiness be going to the United Nations himself?

He smiled again but was noncommittal. "I should like to go on a world tour," he said in a seeming burst of candor. "But always I shall return to India."

The Dalai Lama finally said he had heard I was writing a book on Tibet. The world, he added, should know the truth.

His Holiness spoke throughout in Tibetan, but it was noticeable that he could follow some of the simpler, more direct, questions in English. Apart from the interpreter the only other person present was a junior official of the Indian External Affairs Ministry. On coming in I had presented the ceremonial white silk scarf, but on leaving, His Holiness shook hands warmly. His grip is strong and firm.

I left him with strangely mixed feelings, for the Dalai Lama, while he gives the impression of being acutely unhappy over his country's fate (which indeed he is), also conveys an impression of relief as of one momentarily rescued from oppressive burdens. The mixture of boyishness and maturity, of melancholy combined with an intrinsic gaiety of spirit and charm, is also noticeable.

What has the future in store for him and his country? It is doubtful if he will ever return to Tibet and if the Communists, as long as they rule China, will ever release their grip on his hapless and forlorn land. The Dalai Lama is probably doomed to rove our planet without a visa; but the fate of his country, accentuated by the barefaced repudiation of China's commitments to India on the MacMahon Line, stresses a moral. Communist pledges are no better than pie-crust—made only to be broken.

September 12, 1959   FRANK MORAES

DATE D